THE JOBLESS MILLIONAIRE

THE PATH TO MONEY & TIME FREEDOM OUTSIDE A 9-5

MOA PILLARS

© **Copyright 2021 - All rights reserved.**

The content contained within this book may not be reproduced, duplicated or transmitted without direct written permission from the author or the publisher.

Under no circumstances will any blame or legal responsibility be held against the publisher, or author, for any damages, reparation, or monetary loss due to the information contained within this book, either directly or indirectly.

Legal Notice:

This book is copyright protected. It is only for personal use. You cannot amend, distribute, sell, use, quote or paraphrase any part, or the content within this book, without the consent of the author or publisher.

Disclaimer Notice:

Please note the information contained within this document is for educational and entertainment purposes only. All effort has been executed to present accurate, up to date, reliable, complete information. No warranties of any kind are declared or implied. Readers acknowledge that the author is not engaged in the rendering of legal, financial, medical or professional advice. The content within this book has been derived from various sources. Please consult a licensed professional before attempting any techniques outlined in this book. By reading this document, the reader agrees that under no circumstances is the author responsible for any losses, direct or indirect, that are incurred as a result of the use of the information contained within this document, including, but not limited to, errors, omissions, or inaccuracies

CONTENTS

Introduction — 5

1. EVERY CLOUD HAS A SILVER LINING — 17
   I have a confession to make: — 17
   The Negative Effects of Financial Stress — 19
   Why Employment Isn't As Glamorous as You Might Think — 26
   Why Losing A Job May Be The Best Thing To Have Happened To Anyone — 32

2. YOU CAN DEVELOP IMMUNITY AGAINST JOB LOSS — 39
   Mindset: Abundance vs. Scarcity — 40
   Single vs. Multiple Income Streams — 50
   The Benefits of Entrepreneurship or Business Ownership — 56
   Entrepreneurship Is Less Risky Now — 59
   The Economic Deck Does Not Favor Seekers — 62

3. THE FOUNDATION FOR WEALTH CREATION — 66

4. 7 MONEY SYSTEMS YOU NEED TO KNOW — 93

5. 45 ALTERNATIVE INCOME SOURCES — 113
   Passive Income Streams — 155

6. YOUR ULTIMATE GETTING STARTED GUIDE — 166

7. THE BIGGEST BUSINESS TOOLBOX IN THE WORLD — 183
8. WEALTH ACCUMULATION, WEALTH PRESERVATION, & WEALTH TRANSFER — 192

Conclusion — 203
Discussion Section — 205

INTRODUCTION

I have known Stephen for many years now; he and I met at a neighborhood homeowner's event we hosted, and my first impression of him was that he's a traditional, likable fellow.

Like many of us, he comes from a prototypical American middle-class family. His parents were not wealthy, but they worked very hard to afford a decent living.

As he grew up, Stephen's parents always taught him that to succeed in life, what he needed to do the most was work very hard. Stephen took these values to heart, and since he wanted to be a good son, he obeyed his parents' advice to the letter.

At school, he studied hard and brought home good grades, always coming out at the top quartile of his class. After high school, he received admittance to a top-20 College, and for four years, he pursued a career in Finance where he faired very well.

Not long ago, Stephen graduated, and a top investment bank in the Mid-West hired him immediately. As is customary in the corporate world, Stephen began his career as a low-ranking sales representative for the firm, responsible for attracting new business. It was as good as getting started on a career gets, and Stephen had ambitious dreams.

He hoped that one day, he would become a Class-B Director who works from a pent-house corner office, swiveling around in his Wegner Swivel Chair, as he tends to his exotic bonsai. In his mind, his dream was achievable. After all, he had worked hard and would continue to do so.

Moreover, his bosses often confided in him about their humble beginnings, and always pointed out that he would one day take over one of their roles in the firm.

As the years went by, everything looked good for Stephen. He worked every weekday from 9 to 5 and returned home to his wife, who was expecting their second child.

Every weekend, he would go out on picnics or spend time with friends and family. He had achieved the American dream, a fact he felt good about and proud of all the time. As he often admitted to me every time we went fly-fishing on Sunday afternoons, he felt lucky and was often grateful for his good fortune.

As is usually the case with most of us, Stephen's life has had its fair share of ups and downs. More recently, something unexpected happened.

One Tuesday morning at the beginning of April 2020, Stephen called me with some alarming news. Frantic, he said to me, "Moa, I am losing my mind. I do not know what to do. The pandemic has hit our company hard, and now, my boss has sent me on unpaid leave. I have only three months' worth of expenses in savings. Once that money gives out, I haven't the slightest idea what I'll do next."

Ever since governments around the world enforced lockdowns and other restrictive measures to curb the spread of COVID-19, I have been acutely aware of the fact that many people have lost their jobs, and as a consequence, their incomes. However, despite this knowledge, I never truly appreciated the nature of the situation until my dear friend called me, frantic about the situation.

I figured that if things could go wrong for someone like him, someone who once had a life that was on the fast-track to success, then something must have gone terribly wrong. Further investigation into the matter proved that I was indeed very, very right.

The financial turmoil caused by COVID-19

Sadly, it turns out that the pandemic situation has placed many of us in precarious financial positions that are far worse than Stephen's.

Stephen works in the formal sector, and if his firm doesn't go belly-up because of COVID-19, he may one day get his job back. That realization got me thinking:

What hope is there for those of us who have been working in the informal sector all our lives? What of those of us who freelance and operate in the gig economy? What of those of us who earn just enough to stay alive, and end up living from paycheck to paycheck?

The sad truth is that very few of us can genuinely say that there is some light at the end of this COVID-19 tunnel, especially when it comes to the regular employment situation.

As at the beginning of April, data from the International Labor Organization showed that unemployment reached 14.7%, the highest level since 1948. That means an estimated 23 million Americans are currently out of work.

Keep in mind that this is data from the U.S alone. Around the world, estimates show that a record 1.6 billion people are out of work because of the COVID-

19 pandemic. That's a billion with a b, which is nothing short of horrifying.

Because of this situation, governments around the world have had to step up their efforts to save their economies through measures such as tax relief programs, corporate bailouts, slashing interest rates, printing money, and more. However, such measures are temporary and unlikely to hold up in the long-run. After all, how long do you think governments around the world can sustain the habit of giving their citizenry free money?

Unfortunately, this sad reality is adding to a burden that we all have learned to bear in this post-modern era: intelligent machines taking over most mechanical jobs.

Automation is not helping

The age of computers has led to the proliferation of technologies like Artificial Intelligence, Machine Learning Algorithms, Big Data, the Internet of Things, and other technologies that have significantly reduced human participation in the production process.

We are all aware that technology has been advancing at an almost dizzying rate. We see it all the time.

Now and then, the CEO of a major manufacturing company reports the adoption of a new technology that promises faster production at even lower costs. At Wall Street, for example, today, computers can dig through large amounts of data and give investment firms recommendations in a matter of minutes, if not seconds. Often, such developments mean that people who previously held specific jobs will lose their relevance in the marketplace. It appears that these new technologies will spare almost no one.

Even the production of original art, an endeavor that has for millennia remained in the hands of a select, creative, and capable few, is now possible to accomplish using computers. The Voice of America recently carried a report of a drawing produced by Artificial Intelligence that sold for a cool $432,500.

Investors with deep pockets are quick to congratulate such efforts because such developments often mean doubling, tripling, or even quadrupling their sizable portfolios with little or no work involved. Where does that, however, leave the rest of us who have to work to earn a living?

When we hear such news, they add to that deep sense of fear and insecurity about the future that grips most of us and keeps us turning in our beds every night. What happens when computers and industrial robots replace our need in the labor marketplace?

A recent study conducted by Oxford Economics found that robots will have eliminated over 20 million jobs in the manufacturing sector by the year 2030. For these reasons alone, is it a wonder that mental health experts are reporting increased stress and anxiety?

You see, for most of us, a job is more than just a means of earning a living. For many of us, a job is also a source of identity. A job could be something that gives you purpose and meaning; it could be the one thing that makes getting out of bed each day worthwhile.

When you lose something important, then the results are likely to be a feeling of emptiness, boredom, and a sense of a lack of direction in life. When left to contemplate the many issues of life, you may feel overwhelmed, angry, and hopeless about the future.

Even the uncertainty brought about by thinking about issues like difficulty paying bills, finding food for your family, having to lower your standard of living, etc., can cause a lot of stress and anxiety.

In the face of all this, what should you conclude? That the world has changed? That the idea of job security no longer exists? What's the solution?

You need new answers; you need a new plan; you need a new way of solving your financial problems; you need a new way of seeking financial security; you need to adapt.

Yes, even with everything that has already happened, there's hope, and achieving financial security is still very much possible. Indeed, attaining financial freedom is within your reach, and yes, you can inoculate yourself from the possibility of any future job loss.

ABOUT THIS BOOK

The goal of this book is to give you a roadmap you can follow to do just that.

The book shall show you that despite these challenging times, alternative options, many of which can change your life for the better, still exist. With this book, I hope to show you that there's an abundance of opportunities out there awaiting you, even some you may have never considered before.

The book you are reading details up to 45 possible income sources that you can start and use to attain financial freedom, even during these challenging times. Just think about it: out of 45 possible income alternatives, you only need about one or two to change your life. You can tap into the rest as time and resources allow.

Once you learn about these 45+ opportunities, you'll realize that it's more than possible to find an income source that replaces your job. If you desire to build wealth and finally become financially free, this book will take you by the hand and show you, using a step-by-step approach, how attaining that goal is well within your ability.

The ideas I share in this book are ones that have made my life fabulous and happy beyond my wildest dreams.

ABOUT ME

I am a mother to two beautiful kids and I run a portfolio career; in case you are wondering, a portfolio career is a working style where you combine multiple streams of income. I currently work from home, managing five income streams. In a year, I can earn up to seven figures.

Earning this much has allowed me to purchase a lovely home in a decent neighborhood, to send my kids to the best schools, and to set up a significant retirement package that will allow me to retire comfortably and travel the world.

At times, I look at how far I have come, and I can't believe how well things have turned out for me. Even with the current, mid-COVID-19 economy, I am still doing reasonably well. It's almost as though I am somewhat immune to economic downturns.

You need to understand that my life wasn't always like this.

Not long ago, I was an employee at a child care center. The working hours were long, and the pay was so dismal that supporting my immediate family was a struggle. However hard I tried, I always wound up in debt, living from one paycheck to the other.

All hell broke loose when both my husband and I lost our jobs. I didn't know what to do. I had to figure out something fast. Otherwise, I would stare mournfully at my children starving. No one would employ me at a decent wage since I didn't have any marketable skills or coveted work experience.

Faced with this situation, I decided to go into business for myself. I researched a few options on the internet and started right away, resolutely committed to making it. I worked hard day and night to make sure that things would work out, which they did.

My point is if I can do it, so can you.

IF I CAN DO IT, SO CAN YOU

The benefit you have over me is that you have this book in your hands, which means you can make things work and happen a little bit faster.

You see, I made a lot of mistakes along the way. When I got started, good, well-structured information wasn't easy to find in one place, as is the case with this book.

The fact that you have this book in your hands gives you a better chance than I did.

My promise to you is that by the time you finish reading this book, you will have the knowledge and the means to get your financial life back on track again.

Are you as excited to get started as I am? Good. Let's get started, shall we?

1

EVERY CLOUD HAS A SILVER LINING

"Be willing to take the first step, no matter how small it is. Concentrate on the fact that you are willing to learn. Absolute miracles will happen."

— LOUISE HAY

I HAVE A CONFESSION TO MAKE:

Losing my job a few years ago started a very challenging period in my life. To say things were mighty difficult would be understating it, and when I look back, that period is one of the darkest and most challenging moments of my life.

Everybody agrees that losing a job isn't a good thing. But, for me, it was a little more than that. It was devastating.

I mean, sure, you might look at me today and say that I am doing well for myself. And you would be right. But things weren't always like this.

I still have painful memories from the past. They haunt me now and then. I manage to keep them at bay, but I haven't been able to banish them altogether. I have come to accept that perhaps those memories are there to serve a useful purpose, perhaps to remind me never to take my situation for granted, to work hard, and always stay on top of things.

I'm confessing this to you so that you don't feel alone. I can relate to the situation you are in right now because my situation was painful, scary as hell, and not pretty at all.

THE NEGATIVE EFFECTS OF FINANCIAL STRESS

Here are some of the things I experienced during that trying period of life:

Anxiety

Anxiety is one of the psychological problems I wrestled with every day.

Almost all of us have experienced anxiety at one point or another. But, if you are the rare individual who has no idea what it is, anxiety is a feeling characterized by apprehension in your body and is a result of fear of the unknown. It is a typical physiological response to stress in your body. In medicine, they refer to it as the "fight-or-flight response."

This response occurs when you perceive danger in your environment. The danger can be real or imaginary. In my case, the danger I perceived was the latter: the uncertain future I was facing.

Once the body activates this response, your blood pressure rises, so does your heart rate. You start taking shallow and quick breaths, which delivers less oxygen to your brain. Additionally, your muscles tighten, and as a result, your entire body starts to feel tense, making relaxing a challenge.

During this state of physical arousal, thoughts start occupying your mind almost simultaneously—a phenomenon often called a "racing mind." When your mind is racing, you start playing out mental scenarios of what might happen in the future, in a Hail Mary attempt to find solutions.

Often, these thoughts lead nowhere because they are negative and focused on what has gone wrong with your life instead of the positive, what's great about your life. Negative thoughts often come coupled to negative energy and a lot of emotional anguish. This type of pain is often psychological, but when prolonged, it can get physical.

When your body is in this state of hyper-arousal, it tends to tire very quickly, which is something I experienced quite often. Usually, this happens because the human body cannot sustain the stress response for extended periods.

When I look back, I vividly recall that my energy levels would drop to unimaginable levels, often very early in the day, just a few hours after getting out of bed.

The crazy part is that all this happened before I'd had a chance to accomplish anything. Whatever energy remained couldn't help me do much with the remainder of the day.

That's what happens when you're anxious, especially financially: your life tends to feel stuck.

Depression

I also went through depressive episodes.

It is worth noting that depression and anxiety are first cousins, with the two tending to co-exist in the body. When you are suffering from anxiety, depression usually follows.

You know you're depressed when your mood tends to be low almost all the time. As a consequence, you start to lose interest in doing many things, including those you previously enjoyed.

Depression also affects your appetite. At times you eat very little, and at other times, way too much.

I remember gaining a lot of weight in just a few weeks because eating seemed like an easy way to dull my pain.

When you feel depressed, your life also tends to look blue and meaningless. Your purpose becomes very vague, you start developing self-hate and regret, and you feel worthless, mainly because of embarrassing mistakes you may have made in the past.

Suddenly, nothing about your life seems good. You start to question your existence and begin wondering whether life would be better for those around you if you were not around.

When matters start taking on these dimensions, hurting yourself becomes one of the options under consideration, which makes seeking help vital. I was lucky because I was around people who loved me very much and showed me support.

Isolation

I don't know about you, but there is something about being jobless that made me feel deeply ashamed of myself and inadequate among my cohorts. This feeling of shame made me want to hide my face from the people around me. It made me feel like crawling into a shell forever.

Usually, when you go through a breakup, you rush to your friend and pour your heart out. When you lose a loved one, members of society come together to console you and show support. When you fall ill, you are quick to let your friends know how you are doing. Letting people in during such circumstances always feels natural and quite okay.

Unfortunately:

There's something about losing your primary source of income that makes it a unique type of problem. Maybe it's because of job pride, the loss of financial independence, or the loss of your socioeconomic status.

Whatever the reason, when you lose your job, your problems take an intimate nature. Your self-esteem dips, and you start feeling like a failure, a burden to those around you, all of which makes you determined to hide your vulnerability.

I remember casting my friends aside. For instance, we used to go out on picnics; I stopped attending them. We used to go to church together; I stopped attending church. We used to enjoy barbecues on weekends; I stopped showing up.

Today, I can tell you this: isolation doesn't work. I often felt very lonely, which added to my emotional pain.

Self-doubt

People often talk about how losing a job is not the end of the world. You often hear of stories of men and women who, after a hefty blow, survive the darkest moments of their lives, triumph over them, and who then end up making fantastic comebacks. The popular press loves to tell us such stories.

You hear of successful entrepreneurs who suddenly lost their six or even seven-figure corporate jobs, and whose lives suddenly fell off the proverbial cliff. These people then went on to discover their "true paths in life" and to launch successful careers built on terms they could control.

Such stories are incredible, and we can't help but feel impressed. They are very uplifting, inspiring, and so convincing that they can make us feel like success is a job-loss away. Much of the American dream operates with such stories as its core DNA.

However, when you suddenly become the main character of such a story, it's usually a whole different ballgame. When reality strikes, difficulty, struggle, and fear of the unknown take on real meaning.

For one thing, during these dark moments, self-confidence becomes very hard to come by or practice, and you lose faith in yourself, become doubtful and fearful of your ability to make it.

I remember feeling like an imposter or a fraud, someone not worthy of the past success I had enjoyed—that it had all happened by chance, and I somehow got lucky and wasn't reasonably qualified or a hard worker.

Then I would focus on all the things that went wrong, the mistakes I made, and how all these things led me to my current situation. After that, I would ask myself, "Can I do it again? What if I fail? Is it possible that I am a failure deep down?"

I know this sounds ridiculous, but these are the thoughts I had. Fear of failure can be debilitating. It can stop you in your tracks even before you have begun trying. It takes a strong will to beat back negative tendencies.

As you can tell, what I went through wasn't much different from what you may have gone through at some point, especially as a result of Job loss due to the global pandemic.

Even though my situation was a little bit extreme, I, nevertheless, made it through. You see, it takes someone who has been there to say that making it through anything is possible.

And here something else I realized: A job isn't the best thing in the world after all.

Yes, I am well aware that society makes it look like having a job is one of the ultimate achievements of life because it provides security and freedom from worry. It isn't!

A little digging into the matter revealed some very nasty truths about being an employed person. It's not at all glamorous.

WHY EMPLOYMENT ISN'T AS GLAMOROUS AS YOU MIGHT THINK

For instance, here are a few things you need to be aware of regarding employment:

Overdependence on your boss

Being employed makes you weaker than most people realize.

First, the fact that your means of livelihood comes from your boss leaves you vulnerable, always looking up to your job for almost everything.

In most Western countries (and probably around the world), it is typical to start a family once you come of age and start earning a decent living. This makes it easy to equate your job to almost everything you have in life.

Just think about it:

> Your kid's college tuition, your mortgage, your retirement, and food on the table each day all depend on one person: your boss. He or she becomes the most important person in your life.

And when you think about it, who wants to shoulder all that responsibility? Even worse, what happens when you learn to glorify and give someone else all that power over you? You guessed it right: you open yourself up to abuse.

Is it any wonder that bosses are notorious for placing unrealistic demands on employees and sometimes being downright cruel? And who's to blame for that shameful situation?

If you want to become emotionally stable and independent, you should seek ways to become the boss. Only then can you keep your dignity and self-esteem.

Jobs are not 100% secure

Security is another issue you have to consider: having a job does not guarantee you a lifetime of financial security —at least not as most people would imagine.

Unexpected things can and do happen. Before you know it, you are out of a job and out on the streets again. Even a job in a seemingly stable company still isn't very secure.

Often, corporate executives become reckless, take on ridiculous risks, or even engage in criminal behavior, and such actions end up placing the company's future in a precarious position, and you end up holding the bag.

Consider cases such as the ones involving companies like Enron, WorldCom, Bear Stearns, Lehman Brothers, or even Merrill Lynch. Such companies were major corporate giants.

At one point, Enron was so successful that many people considered it one of the best places to work in America. We all know what happened to all these companies. Merrill Lynch may have enjoyed a reasonably good exit after the Bank of America bought it out at a rock-bottom price, but, as is clear for all to see, a lot of people lost their jobs during the acquisition.

As a general rule, most companies eventually go bankrupt, taking people's jobs along with them. For instance, except for General Electric, all companies listed in the original Dow Jones Industrial Average index in 1896 went bankrupt.

What should that tell you?

It should tell you that if you want to remain in employment, you must always keep in mind that the company you work for may eventually go belly up and that you might lose your job in the process.

Right now, it seems that people are losing their jobs because of the economic impact brought about by COVID-19. However, evidence suggests that layoffs were a common occurrence long before there was even a whisper of this pandemic.

A report released in 2018 by the Bureau of Labor Statistics revealed that more than 3 million people had lost jobs that they had held for at least three years between 2015-2017. The irony is that during this period, Reuters had reported that the economy was doing better than it had since 2005.

Here is the reality: a job will not provide safety, even during a booming economy, end of story!

Less control over your career

Who doesn't like being in control of his or her life? I know I do. I want to be able to control almost everything I can, except for the genuinely uncontrollable forces. Feeling in control gives me a sense of peace of mind that I can't get elsewhere.

However, when employed, you accomplish the exact opposite: you surrender control over your career to someone else.

This person may not share your vision; he or she may not understand your talents, ambitions, dreams, values, and so on. Everything important to you is at the person's mercy.

Take, for instance, something like pay. When you go into employment, you agree to receive a specific sum at the end of the month as a salary. In many cases, this figure isn't as high as you would like it to be.

Further, your compensation does not correlate to performance: no matter how productive you become, there is a ceiling figure on how much you work. That can be disheartening, especially because many people want to earn huge incomes over their lives. With a job, relinquish such ambitions.

And what about tasks? Here, again, there seems to be a discrepancy:

In most jobs, once hired, you get a list of roles to handle. Mostly, these roles are routine tasks that you need to complete on time.

The problem is, you may wish to explore different activities, such as your talents and hobbies. Unfortunately, when restricted and forced to fill your time with pre-determined work tasks, you have little or no time to do anything else creative.

As such, whatever dreams you may have nurtured early in life, dreams of exploring different passions and accomplishing things that matter, take a back seat. They never get to see the light of day until much later when it's already too late to do anything about them. Is this how you would like to live your life?

Lack of freedom of expression

Another problem with most jobs is that by design, many of them project a certain image of the company.

For example, you will find that some companies require employees to wear uniforms during work hours. Others require that you don't adorn yourself with accessories such as earrings, funky hairstyles, and so on.

Therefore, a job, especially a 9-5 one, denies you the freedom to express yourself the way you would like, all for your employer's sake. And most of these rules may have nothing to do with productivity at all.

When you decide to go solo and pursue a personally-defined career path, you get to decide what is and isn't important to you and your business.

It limits the scope of your career

Life in business usually requires people who are multi-talented and experienced. In the services sector, for instance, you will find people who are willing to pay top dollar for someone who has considerable experience and in possession of a variety of skills in a particular niche.

Often clients want to avoid the excessive overhead associated with hiring and managing different people who provide services within a specific domain. It takes a lot of time to do so, and at times, the results of the project may be incongruent with the client's goals.

For these reasons alone, if you are a one-stop-shop for services in your niche, suddenly, you will command better pay and will likely never run out of work. Doesn't that sound good? To me, it does!

Now, as a rule, if you spend much of your productive years at a job, you won't have the opportunity and time to develop different skillsets in your domain. What happens is that over time, you only acquire a few skillsets dictated by your job. Thus, by the time you get around to losing your job or quitting to starting something, you find less demand for your limited skillset in the market.

Therefore, the earlier you create time outside your job so that you can challenge yourself and acquire skills in different areas that matter, the better.

After looking at things from this perspective, you may have realized that losing a job may be the best thing to have ever happened to anyone:

WHY LOSING A JOB MAY BE THE BEST THING TO HAVE HAPPENED TO ANYONE

Here are a few more reasons why losing your job may have been the best thing to have happened to you:

One may have learned that their job wasn't their ideal career path

A job, and the false sense of security that comes with it, has a way of reeling you in and trapping you in its jaws.

It's common to have an idea of what you want to do with your life but still fail to pursue that goal because of the demands of your job.

In other cases, you may live in denial, pretending, and convincing yourself (and others) that you love your job and that you are making a nice living when the truth is that you are very much aware that your true potential lies elsewhere.

Now that you no longer have such an obstacle in your way, you are a free spirit. You can explore whatever your heart desires. Free is good, right?

More time to connect with loved ones

Besides stripping you of considerable earning power, most jobs also rob you of something even much more valuable and irreplaceable: time.

You can make more money, but it limits your time. What if you've exchanged your time for just a little money, all while sacrificing the good times you could be having with those that matter to you the most? Such a bad deal, right?

That's not to say that life as a business owner won't take up time. I am well aware of business people who work extra-long hours. These are people who have decided that more money is worth the extra sacrifice. You may even belong to that category too, which is just fine.

However, the freedom to make your choices without risking your entire livelihood will be yours. I have met a lot of business people who earn a good living doing what they love and have enough time to enjoy life and be with their loved ones.

When you become a business owner, only you get to decide just how hard you wish to work, and how much money will be enough for you, which is a luxury you will never have when working at a 9-5 job. Your boss will only give you ultimatums: you either work a certain number of hours or abandon your career.

An opportunity to acquire more knowledge

It is a known fact that the more you know, the higher your earning potential.

Some jobs, especially those that involve unskilled tasks in the informal sector, can be so demanding that they leave little or no time for study. As a result, you get to watch the whole world change around you as you do nothing to keep up or enhance your economic value.

The good news is that now you have the chance to study, and because of it, an opportunity to engage in work that commands higher pay or have the knowledge to tap into various business opportunities available in the economy today.

That is not to say that going to college is your next option; you don't have to. A college education isn't a requirement for success in the world of business. The truth is that a college education isn't necessary at all; it's good to have, yes, but it's not vital. It's usually costly and has little practical value in the world of business.

The truth is that the world has come a long way. High-quality information related to business is now readily available to anyone willing to seek it and at a low or even free cost. Today, you can read books—like this one—and learn a lot in one sitting than you would learn in 4 years at an expensive business school.

If reading a lot isn't your thing, you can opt to purchase and listen to audiobooks. These days, almost every published book has an accompanying audio version. You can find most at marketplaces like Audible and Scribd.

You can also take business courses taught by experts in every niche you can imagine, with most of these courses being available in digital form. Udemy is a nice place to start. You can study the courses there at any time, place, and using an individual-set pace. Most of these courses offer a lot of value for the money. I owe much of my success to such online courses.

We realize just how much strength we have

You never truly appreciate just how strong you are until you've had the chance to go through a rough time, such as losing a job.

During such moments, you discover the vast inner resources within you that have gone unexploited, resources that can help you pull through super-challenging times. The fact that you are reading this proves that fact.

In the beginning, you probably had thoughts like, "I don't think I can do this. I just don't feel like I can go on." But each day, the sun came up, and you realized that you had just lived through yet another day, and that life has given you another chance to keep fighting.

Despite everything that has happened, you are still here. You are still looking for a way to make things work. That's admirable. You're starting to realize that there's a fire within you, that you should never take your inner strength for granted, and that there is a good chance that things will work out for the best.

You would have never discovered these amazing facts about yourself if you didn't lose your job in the first place. Perhaps you would still be working in that job you hated, collecting a menial paycheck each month, struggling to pay your bills, putting your dreams on hold, and hoping that the worst never happens because you are afraid that you could never handle it. You should be glad that things happened the way they did.

A chance to evaluate the people in our lives

There is something about temporarily falling and failing in life that makes you see things in a better light.

Normally, when things are going great, and life is good, many people masquerade as wolves in sheep's clothing. Friends seem to be in plenty. Everyone seems to be there for you, always around to celebrate your success, and to enjoy the good times: you are never lonely. You start to consider these people true and close friends.

But just how well do you know these people? Just what kind of friends are they? What do you know about their real character?

Unfortunately, you can never judge peoples' trustworthiness when things look good. The moment trouble reveals its head is also the time when the hidden character in people comes out to play. That is the moment when you get to know whether the people you consider friends are ones you can rely on and trust.

What have you discovered about those around you so far? How many of your so-called friends have been supportive? How many have treated you as if you never existed? Are these people you would prefer to keep in your life going forward, or are you just better off sticking with those who are loyal?

It's always good to know what company you keep and who you can count on when it matters the most because, as humans, we are interdependent. You want to know who has your back so that you can have theirs too. There's no better time to arrive at that conclusion than now.

Having accepted that losing your 9-5 job may have been the best thing to have happened to you, it's time to move on and explore how you can develop immunity against income loss:

2

YOU CAN DEVELOP IMMUNITY AGAINST JOB LOSS

"We can create the ultimate job security by becoming less dependent on the organization for which we work and more dependent on our own resources."

— BO BENNETT

After going through job loss, I can only imagine that you never wish for it to happen again in the future; that you never want to end up in such a vulnerable position.

Well, the good news is that achieving such a goal is very much possible, and helping you do this is this book's primary premise.

However, before you can achieve that goal, you have to change yourself fundamentally. No, I don't mean you should stop eating three meals a day, sleeping 8 hours a night, or stop eating junk food—even though that would do your health a lot of good. The change for which I advocate involves looking at the world differently.

Yes, if you want to live in a world where you never have to worry about losing your source of income, you have to change your beliefs and differentiate yourself from the majority. As unbelievable as it sounds, crowd mentality is what got you in this mess in the first place.

Fixing my mindset was one of the first areas I sought to change, and that decision to change is why I'm now where I am. If you wish to follow in my footsteps, you have to make the same changes as well.

Here's how to go about it:

MINDSET: ABUNDANCE VS. SCARCITY

Yes, the first thing you need to change is your mindset.

> One unique thing about life is that you get to choose your beliefs and views, and whatever you choose to believe in dictates the results you get. You see, there is no such thing as right or wrong beliefs; beliefs are either useful or not.

Take, for instance, the abundance vs. scarcity mindset:

How do you choose to look at life? Do you see it as a place of relative scarcity, a place where people have to compete fiercely for whatever is available and where the success of a few means failure for the many, or do you perceive it as a place with plenty for everyone?

Here's the ugly truth:

Most people believe in the scarcity narrative, which explains why the majority of people struggle in life, never taking risks, even when the odds are tremendously in their favor.

The problem with this "herd mindset" is that when you look at matters keenly, you will find that there is often evidence of abundance and that all it takes to get ahead is to acknowledge the availability of plenty of opportunities in this world.

Let's take a simple example like Influencer Marketing, one of the emerging opportunities of the current digital world. We will narrow down our sights to Instagram.

Statista reports that in North America Alone, and for the 2nd Quarter of the year 2019, Influencer Marketing used up a whopping $314 million. That's right, $314 million. Does that sound like little money for a period as short as three months?

You are right; that's no paltry sum. What if you were able to secure just a small portion of that revenue? Would it change your life for the better? You bet it would.

Remember that this represents only a small niche. Countless other industries present similar opportunities.

With that in mind, what would you say about the idea of living in a scarce world? Does it have any merit? NO! And yet, how many people do you hear every day complaining about lacking opportunities?

Keep in mind that this is just but one example. There is so much evidence of abundance in the universe that I could write an entire book on the subject, but let's leave that for another day.

Do you now see why you ought to change your mental orientation to an abundance mindset? Now the question becomes, "How exactly do you go about doing that?"

How to Develop an Abundance Mindset

Here are a few strategic suggestions:

Start thinking big instead of small

The scarcity mindset has conditioned most people to shoot for meager things in life. As a result, only very few people occupy the top spots in any endeavor.

For instance, it's easy to say that you want to make just $50,000 a year in a particular industry or business. The aim sounds achievable and not overly ambitious, right? After all, your goals should be realistic. Wrong!

The truth is that you could as easily earn $200,000 or more putting in the same amount of effort. We can argue that earning $50,000 is a lot harder since you will be competing with a lot more people in the minor leagues seeking equally small and achievable goals.

Here's the deal:

There are more small thinkers than there are big thinkers in this world. Do yourself a favor and position yourself accordingly as a big thinker. If you do so, your journey will be a whole lot easier to travel.

When you have a choice between "thinking big or small," always choose to dream and think as big as you can.

Determine how you can afford it

It's always easier to justify your lack of ability to afford something. As a result, few people ever get the things that they truly want in life. In a way, this stems from the scarcity mindset we just ripped to shreds a little while ago.

> Statements like, "I could never afford that" are dangerous because they encourage mental laziness. They put you in a comfort zone that belittles your ambitions and turns you into a loser. Instead, it is much better to believe you can afford almost anything you want—apart from the truly outrageous—if you put your mind to work.

What do you want? Is it a beautiful home in an upper-middle-class neighborhood? Is it a brand new car? Is it the ability to send your children to the best schools and colleges? Whatever the case, first, believe you can afford it, and then seek ways of affording it.

This book should give you wealth-generation ideas you can use to afford just about anything you've ever wanted.

Don't be afraid of change; welcome and embrace it

Change is inevitable because it's part of nature. Resisting it is nothing but a recipe for mental breakdowns, and whether you like it or not, in the end, the catalyst called change will always win because the world you live in right now is a result of changes that occurred in the past.

Those with the scarcity mindset seek to resist change because they believe that change is painful. How true is that?

Take a look at the world you live in right now. Without a doubt, there are many things you currently enjoy that were never possible a few decades ago—your smartphone is a great example

> The truth is that "change" depends on how you look at it. Change may close down some opportunities, but invariably, new ones open up because of it. You can choose to focus on the negative consequences of change or choose to welcome it and enjoy the positive results that come with it.
> Take, for instance, an endeavor like selling.

In the past, sales and marketing was an activity where those who excelled were those who were truly courageous to face other people and pitch a product to a prospect, often people with charisma and an outgoing personality who could persist even in the face of countless rejections.

Today, I can sit at home, write sales copy on my computer, run inexpensive ads, all the while testing elements that work the best, and from this, generate thousands of dollars in sales in a matter of hours. And I never have to meet or look anyone in the eye—I am introverted, with a shy personality.

Isn't this a positive outcome born out of advancements in technology? Shouldn't I be happy about this new opportunity?

Instead of assuming you already know, embrace learning

Another important step you can take is that of committing to becoming an eternal student.

Start by establishing a never-ending thirst for knowledge; that's what abundant thinkers do. You can never convince yourself that you know enough. Those who think they know everything always have a hard time adapting to what the future brings.

You see, many changes will occur in your lifetime. A lot of these changes will bring new opportunities and challenges. Taping into these opportunities will require knowledge and skill, and you can only achieve that by becoming a continual learner.

Let's go back to the example I just pointed out:

Imagine you are a veteran door-to-door salesperson who has done very well in his career over the past decade or so. Suddenly, you find yourself in a world where consumers are making most of their purchases online.

While this is happening, your income starts dwindling. Where you once used to sell at least a million dollars' worth of product each year, now you're lucky if you can manage to sell $500,000.

You and your employer are worried. He asks you, "Johnny, what is going on? You used to do so well, but now the trend in your sales has been down recently?" You can't explain it. You know something is wrong, but you can't quite pinpoint the exact issue.

Meanwhile, you keep coming across articles from the press profiling stay-at-home entrepreneurs who are raking in millions of dollars in sales each month; these *"kids"* are doing 12 times better than you used to do in your best years.

Growing up, you've never used computers in your work; computers scare you. Even your boss has never felt comfortable around them, and both of you have never perceived the need to learn basic concepts about operating a computer. What's the possible result here?

In a few short years, your boss has no choice but to fire you, citing "lackluster performance." A few months later, you learn that the company went bankrupt and had to close down.

What happened here? It's quite simple.

That is the best outcome you can expect when you refuse to learn new things and get with the times: the world moves on without you.

People who never accept learning new things are the ones who reminisce about how good things used to be once upon a time and complain about how the world has become such an unfair place where a few people take all they can get, leaving nothing for others.

If you want to avoid this fate and sustain your supply of economic opportunities, adopt a lifestyle of constant learning. Then you will never perceive a world with few opportunities on which to capitalize. Instead, your world will become that of endless possibilities.

Focus on what is working instead of what isn't

When things are going slightly wrong, and you are having a hard time getting what you want, what do you do?

Do you focus on what you have lost instead of what you have achieved? Do you focus on what is going well in your life instead of what isn't? Do you count your blessings instead of your failures?

Focusing on the second set of scenarios is what a majority of people only get by and struggle in life.

The truth of the matter is that failure begets more failure. When you allow negativity to run your life, it becomes hard to perceive new opportunities that could turn your situation around.

Start looking at the positives so that you can have the energy and the insight to perceive the endless possibilities around you.

Take proactive steps

Here's another thing you can do.

When presented with a problem, acknowledge its existence, accept it, and start taking steps to make things better.

Don't spend time engaging in an orgy of sorry feelings or mourning a past that is forever gone. Don't spend time worrying yourself into a state of depression, which was my case when my husband and I lost our jobs. As I explained in the previous chapter, when I lost my job, I was a total mess. I couldn't see it back then, but now things are as clear as day.

I have discovered that we waste more time worrying about negative situations than we spend taking positive steps to alleviate the circumstances. That should not be the case. Instead, get up and do something about it.

Yes, things will not change overnight, and you may not find solutions right away, but by taking action, you will be fueling yourself with positive energy and enthusiasm by the mere fact that you are doing something. That alone will stimulate your drive, build momentum, and make you take even more positive steps.

Then with a little success coming your way, your mind will open up and perceive a sea of possibilities that can change your odds dramatically.

Before you can develop immunity against income loss, another change of perspective has to occur in the area concerning income streams.

SINGLE VS. MULTIPLE INCOME STREAMS

Just how many income streams does a person need to become financially secure? Here too, most people have it wrong.

Most people spend most of their lives depending on a single source of income, never stopping to ask themselves just how risky that is.

For most people, the most common source of income is a form of a job of some sort. What're the problems with this approach? You already know the answers, key of which is that at any moment, you could lose your job and find yourself in a desperate income situation.

If there's one common factor amongst most those who have managed to achieve financial freedom, it's that they all have more than one source of income.

For instance, here are some sources of income depended upon by close friends of mine who have achieved millionaire status:

Income from profit

Income from profit is any money you earn from the sale of a product or service. It is typically the compensation you receive above what you spent making the product or service available to a consumer.

Most entrepreneurs make the bulk of their money this way, and you start implementing what you'll learn from this book, it's probable that this is the path you'll follow.

Income from interest

Interest is money earned as compensation for taking the risk to lend someone your money.

Banks and financial institutions have perfected their expertise in this type of business, which is how they've managed to build massive empires. You don't have to be a bank to lend someone and earn interest from the risk taken.

Today, various digital platforms allow people who seek credit for various ventures to find people willing to provide the capital they need—we call this peer-to-peer lending, one of the best ways to make money online today.

If you have a sizeable nest egg, you can build a lending portfolio that earns you a beautiful return from this type of business.

Income from dividends

This type of income is popular among stock market investors. Dividends refer to earnings from a company's economic activities, typically distributed among shareholders.

Dividends are regular among blue-chip corporations, the mature companies that have been around for so long that they've become industry leaders in their respective sectors. Usually, these companies have little room for growth, with the board feeling that distributing earnings among shareholders is more reasonable than re-investing in the business.

If you have savings and can afford to invest a sizeable sum in a company that pays dividends, then you could earn money periodically from doing practically nothing.

Income from rent

Estimates show that 90% of millionaires own some form of real estate that earns rental income. That goes to show that, without a doubt, rental income is one of the most stable sources of investment income there is; after all, tenants have to pay rent each month.

Typically, you won't have the ability to create this source of income unless you earn a very high income already. Rental properties are costly to build or acquire, yes, but that shouldn't stop you. If you follow the advice in this book, a few years down the road, you will have the means to acquire rental real estate.

Income from capital gains

Capital gains income comes from owning appreciable assets such as stocks, bonds, real estate, certificates of deposit, and so on.

It takes some expertise to invest in these assets, and you might have to consult the services of professionals such as CPAs or Tax Attorneys who have wealthy clients who own these types of assets. However, over time and with patience, you could build serious wealth through ownership of these assets.

For instance, consider the case of a company such as Apple. $10,000 invested in this company ten years ago would be worth more than six times as of this writing. Netflix, in comparison, would have earned you more than fifty times that amount.

If you think of those returns, it shall become easier to understand why many wealthy figures are stock market investors.

Income from royalties

A percentage of people I know make their money from earning royalty income, which is income that comes from letting another party use your property.

For instance, let's say you are an author who has written a book you've managed to sell to a publisher. In this case, you receive a sizeable advance, and the publisher retains ownership rights. However, he or she agrees to pay you a certain percentage each month from the sales proceeds of the book. That income is royalty income.

Royalty income can come from other sources such as patents, licenses, copyrighted works, franchises, and others.

As you can see, things are always better for the person who believes and seeks to create multiple sources of income. Generally, the more income sources you have, the better off you shall be in the end.

That, however, is not to say you should branch out into every business imaginable. No, running a business requires knowledge and a level of familiarity that can only come from specializing in a specific niche. Thus, the more specialized you are in a particular area of business, the less likely you are to lose money or go bankrupt.

Nevertheless, you will find that nearly every niche offers several make-money opportunities. Your goal should be to capitalize on as many of those opportunities as possible.

For instance, let's say you've managed to create a blog in a niche such as alternative health. You could earn income from opportunities such as selling eBooks and audiotapes, securing speaking gigs, selling digital courses, offering copywriting services, offering consultancy services, affiliate marketing, selling products, and investing in companies that specialize in that niche.

With such a diversified source of income, you would never worry about what might happen to you at any given point. If one source of income dries up, you would know that you can count on another as you go about finding ways to fix the income stream that has dried up.

Many people focus on the negative aspects of becoming an entrepreneur, never considering the positives, which are usually much significant. People worry about the tough beginnings, the cash flow ups and downs, the probability of failure, and so on.

If you seek genuine financial freedom, you've got to stop thinking of the negatives and start thinking of what good could come out of this decision.

THE BENEFITS OF ENTREPRENEURSHIP OR BUSINESS OWNERSHIP

For instance, you could consider positives such as:

You earn money doing something you love

Making money from a business you love should be a chief consideration. At the risk of sounding like a self-help guru, you are aware that life can be short, right?

If that's the case, why on earth would you opt to do something just for the money? Isn't it better to do something you are genuinely passionate about and get paid at the same time?

Are you the type that believes the extra money is worth it, even though you hate what you are doing? Because here's the deal: <u>roughly 85%</u> of Americans report hating their jobs.

Conversely, Thomas C. Corley, who authored the best-selling book, Rich Habits: The Daily Success Habits of Wealthy Individuals, wrote an article in Business Insider that revealed that 86% of wealthy people like what they do and that 7% love their occupations. Given this, we can argue that 93% of wealthy people like or love what they do for a living.

What should this tell you?

It should tell you that it's usually a myth that rich people have exchanged their happiness for money. The fact is that it's far easier to become wealthy—and happier—doing something that fills you with boundless passion.

You make a difference in people's lives

I'm a firm believer that there is no better way to find meaning in your work than to do work that changes people's lives in a good way. Unfortunately, most people never get the chance to do this.

Most 9-5 job opportunities require workers to complete routine tasks that often mean little to them but that serve the employer's interests; this is one of the reasons why, in general, jobs feel empty.

Even in those rare instances where you end up doing meaningful work, someone else usually ends up taking credit for what you did, which is not a great way to live your professional life.

When you become an entrepreneur, you get to do what you love, and from that, experience for yourself the positive impact you have on peoples' lives. Often, this feeling is more rewarding than even any amount of money you make.

A chance to be a leader

Have you ever wanted other people to look you up? Do you take pride and joy in being in charge of other people instead of the other way round?

Perhaps you wish to become a public figure or get elected to public office one day. If so, then becoming an entrepreneur is one of the best ways to actualize that wish.

As a business owner, you can grow to the point of hiring people to work at your enterprise. You could help people realize their full potential or actualize their dreams of a successful career. Could you imagine anything else being that rewarding?

You build a network of like-minded individuals

You might think that being an entrepreneur is a solitary pursuit that often leads to loneliness. You'd be wrong, and nothing could be further from the truth.

Sure, it might feel that way during those early years when you're just getting started, but later, especially when you start faring well, things change, and you get a chance to meet people motivated by the same reasons that drive you.

You can exchange ideas, share thoughts, even formulate strategies, and even exchange contacts; there's a robust support system among business people.

In some cases, you will meet people who have achieved higher levels of success or people with access to vast resources and even more powerful connections. These people will encourage you to do better, and you could even end up securing business opportunities from them.

ENTREPRENEURSHIP IS LESS RISKY NOW

A widely known fact was that entrepreneurship was a risky endeavor that only a brave few attempted. Even today, most people hold such opinions.

The truth, however, is that the world has come a long way. Things are a lot better than they used to be. Today, technology has made it a whole lot easier to go into business without taking on considerable risk.

Today, things are the opposite of what they to be. Today, it's riskier to be an employee than it is to go into business for yourself: the economic deck seems stacked against job seekers.

Recent practices adopted by those in the world of business have created problems for people with an employee-orientation, problems no one could have envisioned just a few years ago.

Take, for instance, a recent business practice like outsourcing, a practice where a company prefers to hire a workforce from emerging economies where standards of living are much lower. Today, many businesses outsource key business functionalities as a way to reduce operating costs and also drive down the cost of products and services marketed to consumers.

For instance, consider a job like Information Technology. According to data from Payscale, an IT worker in the U.S earns $79,371 a year. Comparatively, a worker in China or India may be more than willing to accept $8,400 or $7,000 a year, respectively. Moreover, workers in these countries are often more skilled than those in the U.S.

This situation presents an extraordinary opportunity for technology companies in the U.S. They can cut their costs, significantly enhancing their chances of profitability, all while reducing the cost of goods and services sold to American consumers.

Another practice is that of automation. We have already talked about how AI-driven robots are taking over business roles that involve manual and repetitive tasks because they can accomplish the same amount of work faster and more efficiently. Think of all the people who will lose their jobs simply because a robot can assemble a car at a much faster rate.

As if that's not enough, evidence suggests that businesses are starting to rely on freelance workers instead of full-time employees. Currently, the number of freelancers stands at 57 million. By 2027, estimates show that freelancers will make up half of the entire American workforce.

There are many reasons why companies may wish to hire freelancers instead of full-time employees. The chief reason is the opportunity for cost reduction, and businesses love reducing costs, especially when it represents a chance for profitability and competitiveness.

Given the global nature of the current economy, expectations in the business world are that modern practices like these will only increase. That's why no business is likely to maintain old methods that are likely to bankrupt it or make it less competitive in a marketplace filled with businesses employing such practices.

Do you remember the adage, "If you can't beat them, join them?" That's why I hold on to the notion that it's riskier to hold on to being an employee for life. Even if you were to get a job today, you would never feel secure when the prospect of your company adopting practices that make your role obsolete hangs over you.

On the flipside, conditions favor those who are willing to become entrepreneurs or self-employed professionals. When you do, you have access to cheap labor, technologies that drive costs down, and a global market that will consume your products and services.

Yes, it's a lot more attractive to have options like these. You can take your shot and sleep like a baby at night, knowing that the odds of you failing are much less than those of you succeeding.

THE ECONOMIC DECK DOES NOT FAVOR SEEKERS

To drive my point home, we are going to look at two people: Jerry and Mark.

In 2010, Jerry and Mark graduated from a prestigious university with honors in accounting. Both quickly got started in the business world roughly at the same time after a major alcohol producer hired them both. But there was a difference:

Jerry was always ignorant of what happened around him. Like most people, he believed in the old narrative of playing it safe and getting a safe and secure job for life. Therefore, he convinced himself that he had achieved his main goal in life and that all he needed to do was focus on his job while rest took care of itself.

Mark, on the other hand, wasn't so naïve. He was always vigilant and suspicious. He had learned that friends close to his father had lost jobs that they had held for 30 years. He was keen on investigating what circumstances led to this unfortunate situation.

Furthermore, as an avid reader of the Wall Street Journal, he had read many articles suggesting that companies were adopting new business practices designed to help them remain competitive in the current global market.

He knew, for instance, that for jobs that didn't pertain to the main business, companies were laying off full-time staff and hiring freelancers. Even better, he knew that his job fitted that category.

Determined to minimize his perceived risk of failure, Mark sought to hedge his bet. He figured that he would take on freelance accounting assignments on the side as a way to supplement his income and shield himself against job loss. To his surprise, his "side duties" were consistent and well-paying.

Meanwhile, Jerry was getting comfortable at his job. Other than investing in his 401k, he wasn't doing much to secure his future.

For various years, things looked good for both men. Jerry secured several promotions that came with increased pay. Mark did well, but not very much, considering that he was only putting in the required hours at his job and heading home to carry out his freelance gigs.

Last year, the unexpected happened.

The company underwent some financial problems, with new management brought in to clean up the mess. The company's orientation changed overnight.

After refusing to renegotiate a lower pay, the new boss promptly eliminated Jerry's overpaid position. The boss was unfazed as he did this. As it turned out, he had received an offer from a retired professional in the Philippines who had considerable experience and was willing to settle for half the pay Jerry was receiving.

Mark, on the other hand, could afford to receive lower pay, because of which he could retain his job. He felt OK with lower pay because, after all, he was earning a lot of money from his side business. However, he thought of all the stable connections he had established and his gold chain reputation for quality work.

At that point, his "side business" had grown to the point of earning for him more than five times what his salaried position paid. He saw no logic in staying on with the company and quickly resigned so that he could go into business full time.

Ask yourself this: Who would you like to be?

Would you like to be Jerry, who lost his job and was now on the streets without a plan, or would you prefer to be Mark, who was all too happy to resign so that he could focus on his business? You know the correct answer!

3

THE FOUNDATION FOR WEALTH CREATION

"If we command our wealth, we shall be rich and free. If our wealth commands us, we are poor indeed."

— EDMUND BURKE

Let's start by laying the foundation for the change that is about to come, the change that will turn you into an economic success.

You see:

Making money isn't mysterious. Contrary to what most people assume, wealth creation doesn't involve magic, dumb luck, robbing people, or winning the lottery. Making money is not accidental.

Creating wealth is a matter of following some basic, but classic principles that have proven to work over the ages. The more you follow these rules with discipline, the easier your journey to becoming wealthy becomes.

Those who have money—and I am not talking about people who act rich at the expense of being genuinely wealthy—follow these principles to the latter.

Dr. Thomas J. Stanley dedicated his life-long career to studying millionaires in America for over 40 years. He found that his wealthy respondents followed classic wealth building principles.

It is funny how many people think that wealthy people inherited their wealth. People imagine that the wealthy are descendants of the Rockefellers, the Medicis, the Fords, the Morgans, or the Vanderbilts.

Yet, Dr. Stanley revealed that this widespread assumption was at odds with his research findings. He explained that most such generations have already depleted most (if not all) of their wealth.

In contrast, he determined that most millionaires never came from wealthy backgrounds or inherited even a dollar of their wealth. Further, for those whose parents were wealthy, he found that some of these parents (roughly 40%) didn't believe in passing along wealth. Just read The Millionaire Next Door.

Another prevalent bias is that rich people have high-status occupations that pay a lot of money. Think of all the rock stars, the Wall Street Gurus, the distinguished Hollywood megastars, the footballers, the golfers, the doctors, the lawyers, and the like. These must be the only rich people in America, right?

As a result of believing this, most people are keen on becoming such high-income earners. People dream of six or even seven-figure incomes. And for those who realize the extraordinary demands of such careers, it seems that wealth is just an unattainable goal.

Yet, Dr. Stanley found that many wealthy people didn't occupy high-status occupations. Most never earned significant incomes or wages from fancy corporate titles. He found that most people who display high status both in their lifestyles and occupations were not wealthy.

Instead, he discovered millionaires among scrap metal dealers, fishers, owners of factories, rice farmers, teachers, dry cleaners, self-employed professionals, and owners of janitorial firms.

Moreover, almost none ever played or won the lottery in their life. You are more likely to experience a lightning strike before you ever make money from the lottery. These wealthy people simply began from scratch and worked their way up.

What should this tell you?

It should tell you that most wealthy people are ordinary people. They became wealthy and stayed that way by following classic wealth-building principles.

You have within you the power to become a millionaire next door; all you have to do is follow the same money principles we shall talk about later in this guide; they are the cornerstones of creating wealth.

These rules are unbreakable. You can only hope to break yourself against these rules. And when you do that, you will suffer the ultimate consequence of going broke and staying that way.

It is important to note that there's nothing new about these rules. You probably hear about them every time you read about money because, yes, they are that commonplace and trite.

Yet, they are profound, with their profoundness coming from the fact that most people manage to break them every time, only to wind up in financial trouble.

Here they are:

Rule #1: Master Budgeting

> *"A budget is telling your money where to go instead of wondering where it went."*
>
> — DAVE RAMSEY

"Budget your money" is probably one of the most well-known wealth-creation advice that you probably can't stand to hear one more time.

Nevertheless, I feel that I should discuss it in this book because the attention most people give it is inversely proportional to its importance in their lives.

You can earn a lot of money, but if you never budget for it down to the very last penny, you are likely to face financial problems.

People say, "Budgeting sounds like a good idea. I'll do it someday," but then procrastination sets in, and they never do it.

That happens because budgeting is not fun: nothing about carefully squeezing dollar amounts to categories of expenses feels good. Millionaires who budget also don't feel good about it either; only a rare few enjoy the budgeting process.

There are, however, far worse things, like waking up 10 or 20 years from now and realizing that you've gotten nowhere in life, despite working so hard or realizing that you have nothing set aside for retirement and that you will have to work well into your old age.

Here's something you need to know about life in general:

Doing things that feel good isn't usually the best approach to life. Neglecting important activities while only seeking momentary emotional satisfaction won't serve your best interest in the long run.

With this in mind, let me ask you this. Do you have a budget?

If you do, then congratulations. Feel good about yourself because you are among the few who do. However, if you don't, I urge you to stick with me and draft one as you read this section.

What's the best way to get started on the budget-creation process?

Here's how:

How to Budget Like A Pro

First:

Step 1: Determining your reasons

You begin by first setting goals because having a clear goal motivates you to create a budget and stick to it. In life, it's easier to accomplish difficult things that require hard work and discipline if you have a clear purpose in mind.

That's why you should start by asking yourself what main advantage you will get out of organizing your finances and creating a budget. Do you wish to retire in comfort? Do you want to send your kids to a prestigious university? Do you wish to buy a home in a quality neighborhood? Do you wish to pay off your $150,000 student loan? The reasons will vary from one person to another.

Whatever that case, make sure your reason—or more than one—is as strong as possible. If your reason is weak, you will falter along the way and fall back to your old, money-gobbling habits.

Step 2: Determine your expenses

After nailing down your *WHY*, the next step is to establish what you spend your money on in a typical accounting period. There are many ways you can go about this.

For instance, you can look through your bank statements, collect all your receipts and go through every last one of them, or determine which purchases you made and whether they fit into certain categories.

At the very least, you should come up with a list of items that looks more or less like the one below:

- Rent/Mortgage
- Utilities, which include gas, water, electricity, internet, phone, and others
- Credit payments
- Groceries
- Entertainment
- Insurance
- Subscription services
- Taxes

Once you have a list, try categorizing the items into needs and wants. Doing this helps you separate essential expenses from the trivial ones that you can do without, especially if you're hemorrhaging money. This way, it will be much easier to determine where you can begin cutting costs accordingly.

Step 3: Determine your income

Next, you want to determine exactly how much income you have coming to you.

You should already know this intuitively. However, if you receive income from a wide variety of sources, or if your income varies from one month to the next, you will want to establish a good estimate of what your income looks like within a specific accounting period.

A good thing to do in such a scenario would be to add up your income from several sources and obtain the average. The number you come up with should be your basis when creating a budget.

Step 4: Determine how much you spend

You have added up all your expenses and now have a good idea of what you make each month. What have you learned so far about your finances?

Are you living above your means, in debt, or do you have plenty left over after spending? Whatever you uncover should dictate what steps you will take next.

This step is the point where most people receive a shocking revelation about their situation. For many, "Mmmmh… I am not doing as well as I thought," is a common response to this step.

If you can relate to this, then the steps that follow will help you a great deal.

Step 5: Find opportunities for cutting back

Once you have determined the realities of your financial situation, it's time to find ways of cutting back and saving money.

Cutting back is easy to do once you have categorized your expenses into wants and needs. Needs are things you can't do without in your life; they are pretty basic and fall into roughly four categories:

- Food
- Shelter
- Clothing
- Healthcare

Given that these expenses are basic, you want to make sure they remain that way. Ask yourself whether the figures around these categories seem inflated. For instance, do you feel it's okay to spend $1000 on food or $2500 on rent? Does it sound ridiculous? If it does, seek ways to minimize that expenditure.

Here are some suggestions to try:

- **If your rent is too high, consider relocating to a cheaper neighborhood.** Rent prices and rates rent are often about the hype related to inflated market values more than the quality of the housing itself. That is usually the case in metropolitan areas.
- **If you are living in or close to a city, especially around people who are earning very high incomes, you're probably paying very high rent or mortgage rates, all for the pride of living in such areas.** And let's not even talk about the pressure to consume at a level that matches or even competes with your good-looking neighbors, the Joneses. Relocating to someplace where the cost of housing is reasonable, and your neighbors generally earn less than you do, could be the best decision you will ever make regarding your money.
- **Consider shopping for food in bulk.** Buying food from wholesalers usually comes at a steep discount, with the food generally consumed for much longer, thereby translating into substantial savings.
- **Avoid shopping for clothes at expensive stores and, instead, go to discount stores.**

Purchase clothing from Walmart, Macy's, or JC Penny instead of Nordstrom, Hickey Freeman, Neiman Marcus, Saks Fifth Avenue, or Lord and Taylor. Focus on buying quality clothing at reasonable prices instead of showy style.

- **Buy clothes that are machine washable** instead of those that need dry-cleaning. The fees you pay at the dry-cleaner can eat into your income.

When it comes to wants, that's where you have the biggest opportunity to cut back and reduce your cost.

As a rule, wants are things you don't need. They just enhance your standard of living or cater to your desires. For these reasons, reducing your wants present you with a rare chance to become extremely frugal—for your finances' sake.

Here's why:

Often, purchases around what you want only satisfy your emotions. Perhaps it's a pricey vacation, a diamond-encrusted watch, an expensive and nice-looking car, subscriptions to entertainment services like Netflix, Cable TV, Amazon Prime, Hulu, and the like. These are things you can eliminate from your budget or substitute with less expensive options.

Overall, spending money (especially on things) only leads to temporary excitement, not actual happiness. Happiness is not something you can buy. Most millionaires interviewed by Dr. Stanley agreed that the best things in life are free—or at least priced reasonably.

Step 6: Allocate money efficiently

During the budget creation process, the last thing you need to do is figure out a way to distribute the money you make in a new way that will provide for you adequately without depriving yourself.

Yes, you want to be frugal and economical with how you use your resources, but at the same time, you don't want to put yourself through pain and misery. Spending money responsibly and well is an act of balance.

> Think of money as you would food.

We can all agree that eating too much and often in the wrong ways is likely to lead to health problems and weight gain. Minimizing your intake is usually advisable.

What does the average person do when he or she wants to lose weight? They starve and deprive themselves of their favorite foods as a way to lose weight quickly. What then happens? The person loses some weight in the short term but later embarks on a dangerous bingeing spree that makes them gain more weight than they lost before.

Instead, a balanced regimen of reduced food intake, coupled with exercise, would have worked better in the long-term. Unfortunately, most people don't have long-term horizons in their pursuit of goals.

With money, you could do the same: avoid spending money at all, living like a monk and dressing like a homeless hipster, only to go back to your old habits later, big time.

Instead, allocate money in a way that allows you to supply yourself with the basics without going crazy, all while saving and allowing some money on the side to enjoy yourself and indulge occasionally. You could develop any number of ways to do this, but I have two favorite models to help you figure out this mess. They are:

The 50/20/30 method

This model is very straightforward: You direct 50 percent of your take-home pay to basic and essential expenses like food, shelter, clothing, and so on.

Then, you set aside 20 percent to savings, investments, and debt-reduction plans. Lastly, you allow yourself the remaining 30 percent for non-essential personal expenses—things like entertainment, fancy dinners with your spouse, cool gadgets, and the like.

Most people do well with this program.

The 60/20/20 method

This method is a slight modification of the one above.

You set aside 60 percent to basic expenditure, 20 percent to savings and investments, and the remaining 20 percent to personal expenses.

This method works best for people who feel a little guilty for spoiling themselves too much, all while not holding down their major expenses comfortably in the process.

After you have followed these basic steps, you will want to prepare a document that makes your budget official.

If you prefer digitized as I do, you may want to use a spreadsheet program like excel, which has many templates that can help you prepare a household's budget based on the guidelines mentioned above.

You can also go the old fashioned way and create a budget on a sheet of paper. Whichever way you do it is fine.

Rule #2: Save

After discussing the concept of budgeting, you probably appreciate the importance of saving money whenever possible. After all, a portion of your budget demands that a portion of your income should go into savings.

Saving is what many financial experts call *"paying yourself first."* Before you pay the owner and operator of the discount store, the landlord, the bank, or the restaurant owner, set aside money for yourself first; otherwise, you will go broke.

What's a good rule about saving?

Put aside at least 10% of your monthly income, then spend the rest on other things.

If you want to increase your ability to save, you will have to be creative. There are several opportunities to save money, especially among expenditures. We discussed a few, but here are other options you may wish to explore:

Skyrocket Your Savings With These Strategies

To save more, focus on:

Food

We all have to spend money on food. However, there are various options you can explore to save money. They include:

- **Cooking meals at home:** Sadly, and despite being fun, eating out can get expensive. Few people can afford to eat out every time without putting a significant dent on their monthly income. Instead of eating out all the time, seek ways to prepare most of your meals at home. The real motivation should be that restaurants don't offer much in terms of value. Nearly all the meals prepared at a restaurant are ones you can cook and have at home for more half the cost
- **Avoid bottled water:** Bottled water isn't always of superior quality, and the price isn't usually justified. It's always a better idea to drink tap water; if you feel concerned about pathogens, boils your water.
- **Avoid beverages at restaurants:** When you do eat at restaurants, try as much as possible to stay away from beverages if you can. Most restaurants make their profits from overpriced drinks. It's better to buy drinks elsewhere where the price is lower or prepare them at home

Cars

If you are not careful, Cars can also be money pits. Here are some rules to consider:

- **Research before buying a car:** A car usually costs more than most people can imagine, and some people have no business purchasing a vehicle at all. Before you buy a car, consider costs such as insurance, monthly payments, repairs, fuel, as well as the sticker price. If the number scares you, either purchase a cheaper car or avoid buying a car altogether.
- **Avoid leasing or financing:** When it comes to buying a car, the best thing you could ever do is pay cash. Financing is always a sign that you can't afford whatever you are buying. Generally, leasing is an expensive option that you should avoid.
- **Buy used cars:** Besides prestige, there's seldom a good reason to buy a new car. You can usually find a good deal on a used car because cars tend to depreciate rapidly. If you insist on buying a car, at least try to get a used one that is in good condition.

Clothing

Since you have to spend money on clothing, here are some things to try:

- **Avoid the latest fashion:** Fashion fads are a way for marketers to encourage you to spend more of your money on clothing, and before

you know it, you have spent a fortune on "looking trendy." Instead, purchase quality classic clothing that never goes out of style.
- **Reduce accessories:** Accessories such as jewelry, handbags, and so on are good to have. However, people, especially women, tend to splurge on these artifacts. Think about it, do you need ten handbags? Be reasonable, and purchase what you need.

Fun

Entertainment is good because it adds to the joy of living and keeps life from being monotonous. However, you must watch out by observing the following:

- **Seek free or low-cost entertainment:** Spending a lot of money on having fun isn't always justified. How much does it cost to go for a walk in the park or the mall? How much will it cost to play a video game or watch a movie at home? How much will it cost to visit your son at school to watch him play football? Probably very little, and yet, you will get a lot of satisfaction from these activities.
- **As for gadgets, keep from being the first one to buy the latest model.** Gadgets, especially smartphones, debut at inflated prices that tend to decline rapidly after a year or two.

Additionally, early models have defects that manufacturers usually fix in units that hit the marketplace later.

Addictive habits

Certain habits can become costly both in terms of your money and health. Do your best to curb them. They include:

- **Smoking:** Smoking cigarettes increase your risk of lung cancer. Additionally, smoking is also costly. For instance, estimates indicate that an average smoker can easily consume a pack in a day. At $6 a pack, that amounts to over $21,900 in 10 years. What if you invested that money for 30 years at a rate of 8 percent compounded annually? It would amount to $220,372.19. If that doesn't convince you to quit smoking, I don't know what will.
- **Alcoholism:** Besides impairing your judgment and destroying your liver, alcohol costs money. Calculations concerning alcohol are similar to those involving cigarettes, with the primary difference being that because liquor is costlier, the numbers are much worse. Just ask yourself whether you prefer to fritter away your wealth, only to risk dying of liver cirrhosis.
- **Gambling:** Gamblers, as a rule, generally lose

money. You see, most casino games have a negative mathematical edge, which makes losing money playing these games is a mathematical certainty, especially if you play long enough. Yet, the occasional wins often enchant ordinary people, leading them to think that playing these games is a good idea. It takes a sophisticated math genius to play and win these games. Do you fit that description? Since you're most likely not, quit gambling: it isn't worth it.

These techniques should drive home a fundamental principle about handling money: always live below your means. Keep from joining the crowd that is hell-bent on consumption.

High consumers often look rich, but looks being what they are, disguise the fact that these people often have little or no wealth in real dollar terms; most are in debt. Never admire these people or aspire to become like them.

Rule #3: Invest Your Savings

Saving money is good, but it isn't enough. You need to invest the money you save so that it works for you. I have never met a wealthy person who works and saves money for the sake of saving; almost all of them save so that they can invest their money in some way or the other.

Unfortunately, when most people think of investing, they counter with the argument, *"I don't have money to invest."*

When you think about it, this argument seems logical; after all, we all seem to be under the impression that it takes a lot of money to make money in the investment world.

When CNBC interviews some top investment banker who is managing billions of dollars at some hedge fund or some analyst who gets paid six figures salary a year to make investment predictions, the silent message seems to be, "Only those who are wealthy can afford to play this game called investing."

That is only a half-truth:

The fact of the matter is that times have changed. Technology, as well as government policies affecting the world of finance, have created vast pools of opportunities, even for those with little money to play.

For instance, in the past, you could only purchase a stock at the market price and pay a flat commission on the spot. Today, you can purchase fractional positions in the market.

For instance, if the stock price of Company A is selling at $300 and all you have is $50, a retail broker can allow you to purchase 0.02 lots. In the old days, such an arrangement wasn't an option. You had to purchase a full lot.

That means today, even if you have a small amount of capital to start, you can still play and win. Further, here's something else to consider: a small amount of money shouldn't discourage you as long as you have the power of compound interest by your side.

Let's say you invest $500 in an investment vehicle that pays 10% interest annually. Let's also assume that during this time, you commit to saving at least $50 each month to add to your investment. That amounts to $600 per year. In 30 years, you will have amassed $117,290.76, which is nothing short of a small fortune. This conservative plan illustrates the power of growing a seemingly small amount into enormous portions.

What if you were able to double, triple, or even multiply your investment per year ten times down the road? Can you see how possible it is to become wealthy by starting small and following a simple plan?

The point is simple: however small an amount you have, save it and invest it; you'll be glad you did because money is like seeds. You can eat or sow the seeds. When you realize that seeds can grow into corn that fills an entire farm, you will say NO to the urge to eat them.

We'll cover investment opportunities and ideas later. For now, I hope that you get the idea.

Rule #4: Get Out Of Debt

Most genuinely wealthy people understand something simple: debt is a burden and a huge impediment to building wealth and becoming financially free. Dave Ramsey always says, "The borrower is a slave to the lender." I agree.

Getting into debt is often a bad idea and even so-called "good debt" is not always a wise idea. Consider a debt such as a mortgage, often considered a good idea since you are borrowing to invest in a property that has the potential to appreciate. The government, however, estimates that 250,000 families have their homes foreclosed upon every month.

> Debt is an anchor that keeps you from getting ahead financially. Even Warren Buffet opposes it. He once said, *"If you are smart, you will make a lot of money without borrowing."*

Given the damaging impact of debt, what should you do? The answer is simple:

Prepare a plan that helps you get out of debt as soon as you possibly can because debt is a major threat to your financial freedom. If you learn nothing else from this book but how to get yourself out of debt, I will consider the book a raging success.

As you can imagine, and like most things, there are several approaches to getting out of debt. For some people, getting out of debt can be as simple as setting aside some money each month to pay it off. For others, it may involve a sophisticated plan of action that involves strategies like consolidation, analyzing interest rates, prioritizing payments, consulting credit counselors, and so on.

The topic is complex, with entire books written about it. By far, my best pick is The Total Money Makeover by Dave Ramsey, a world-renowned authority who has helped millions of people get out of precarious financial situations through a sound approach. You would be wise to listen to him.

Rule #5: Set Up An Emergency Fund

Here's another thing you have to keep in mind at all times. The moment you get out of the current situation and start making money again, be sure to set aside some money for emergencies.

An emergency fund is a fund dedicated to fixing unexpected financial problems. Can you remember the story of my friend Stephen that I told at the start of this book? Stephen was wise to have an emergency fund in place. If he didn't, things might have been much worse for him.

Life has a pesky habit of throwing surprises our way. You might fall seriously ill, your car might break down, or you might lose your primary source of income. The possibilities are endless.

Since you never know what might hit you, it helps to prepare somehow. This way, even if some emergency happens, you can survive the inevitable crash without getting into deep financial trouble or emotionally destroying yourself.

Now, one thing you should notes is that the bigger the emergency fund, the better. As a general rule, however, if you are a self-employed person, a fund with roughly six months' worth of expenses should be your minimum. If you are an employee who has a predictable cash-flow, a fund with three months' worth of expenses is passable.

The data from your budget should give you a good idea of how much you need to have in your emergency fund. Once you have a figure, strive to set come up with that amount as soon as possible.

However, if you feel overburdened by debt, then you might need to employ what Dave Ramsey has always recommended: set aside $1000 in your emergency savings account before you proceed with everything else. It isn't enough, but it can act as a temporary cushion. Afterward, you can fill it with the appropriate amount.

You must keep your emergency fund/account fully funded at all times. If something comes up and you have to spend some money from this fund, be sure to replace it.

Also, remember to keep the money in an easily accessible account. Usually, a high-yield savings account is a good option. You won't build wealth from the interest earned, but that isn't the point. The idea is to be able to access your money without going through hoops or having to pay significant penalties.

Now that you have the basics of money management under your belt, in the next chapter, we will move on and talk about 7 money systems you need to know:

4

7 MONEY SYSTEMS YOU NEED TO KNOW

"The key is to work extremely hard for a short period (1-5 years), create abundant wealth, and then make money work hard for you through wise investments that yield a passive income for life."

— H.W. CHARLES

This primer chapter discusses actual money-making strategies you can deploy. The truth is that opportunities are endless, but before you can take advantage of them, you need to understand the bigger picture because it helps give structure and organization to income opportunities so that you can position yourself accordingly.

Perhaps you want to work from home, or you prefer meeting people in person. Perhaps you have a technological background you can leverage to your advantage. Maybe you have resources at your disposal that can give you a head start. All these factors determine which opportunities to choose and exploit.

For these reasons, we are going to look at 7 primary income systems that form the basis of everything else. They include:

Technological Systems

We live in an era greatly influenced by technology, with many of the changes in the modern world occasioned by technology. Thanks to technology, a lot of things are now easier than they have ever been.

For instance, technology has made it easier for small businesses to perform in-house accounting without hiring a professional who may charge expensive fees. Industrial robots can assemble cars in a fraction of the time it takes humans to do the same amount of work. Technology has exposed new marketing channels that have given businesses a chance to reach customers in better and more efficient ways.

Look at how technology has affected even a piece of work like the book you are currently reading. You are probably reading this book from a PC, a laptop, or even a smartphone.

That is how prevalent technology is: almost everyone today uses it, which is why technology offers a tremendous opportunity for you to make money by going into business for yourself. Technology is in demand, and given how well we've taken to it, it will always be.

You may want to go into the business of selling the latest technological gadgets that people use in business. If that's the case, you can count on there being a ready market for such devices.

One of my friends specializes in selling technology products. Each month, he receives tenders from various organizations in the private and public sectors. Recently at the beginning of the Covid-19 fiasco, he requested my help in finding a supplier for a large number of computers and related accessories for a high-value client.

As I prepared an invoice after receiving estimates from my contacts, I couldn't believe the quoted amount: It was more than $200,000, but my friend looked at the figure and said, "That's okay." Later, I learned that he rakes in roughly $10,000 each month from his operation. How cool is that?

You don't have to sell tech gadgets to make money. Expertise in technology is in high demand. You can be a programmer, a web designer, an artificial intelligence expert, a machine learning expert, a user experience designer (UX), and so on.

I know people who take home thousands of dollars each month selling their services in each of these sectors. And almost all of them work from home. Some didn't even go to college to acquire these skills. Some just benefitted from free or inexpensive courses offered on platforms like Udemy and EdX.

You may want to look deeply into this area. I smell massive opportunities in the future, especially with the rapid change in the world today. Even Forbes predicts a high potential in this area.

Content Systems

Another lucrative opportunity you may want to look into has to do with the content creation.

By content, I mean information of some sort that people interact with in one way or the other. Content can take many forms. There is video content such as the one you see on platforms like YouTube, Instagram, and Facebook. Then there is written content such as the one you find in books, blogs, magazines, whitepapers, newspapers, reports, and so on.

You also have content that takes the form of pictures, infographics, and presentations. In all, content is diverse, which is a good sign that shows the plentifulness of opportunities in content creation.

Why create content? What's the value of it? What should make you certain that your investment in this area will be worth your while?

Well, first, it helps to understand that information will always be in demand. There is always someone somewhere who wishes to know more about something. That, dear friend, is a ticket to opportunity.

For instance, we can classify the book you are reading right now as content. You are reading it because you wish to know more about making money. The good thing is that you don't have to write books on making money alone. People have many other unique and more pressing problems in their lives.

Perhaps someone is having problems with dog training, navigating the dating arena, or cooking a certain meal. You can create an informational product that helps the person get around that problem, thereby earning yourself a good income.

Secondly, high-quality content has great marketing value. In today's world, people wish to know more about something before they can do business with you. For instance, if I wish to purchase a new TV, I may want to know about the latest features included in TV sets, the various things I can do with that TV, and how to avoid problems.

I may also want to know about related gadgets I may need to purchase to enjoy my TV, the best place to mount it on my wall, the various models available, the best pick, and so on. The most authoritative source that provides this type of information will also likely be the person I trust with my business; this isn't mere talk.

Companies are finding that compared to traditional marketing, taking a content-based approach is more effective, cheaper, and translates into more sales. Thus, you can receive a handsome payment to create content strategies for businesses.

Neil Patel is a renowned content marketer. From his consulting firm, I'm Kind of A Big deal Inc, he earns several million dollars each year and has worked with household names such as Google, Uber, Yahoo, Amazon, and so on.

You can follow his footsteps and provide content marketing services to smaller companies or those within a specific niche.

Rental Systems

You can also earn great money from renting. By renting, I mean making property, a product, or a service available for temporary use by other parties at a fee.

If you live in a house where you pay rent each month to the owner, you're familiar with this concept. The property owner makes money because you are using his or her property.

Besides residential properties, renting can apply to many other things. You can rent out your car, construction tools such as a cement mixer, or intellectual properties such as a movie or a computer program. Other items you can rent out include washing machines, television sets, boats, airplanes, bicycles, clothes, handbags, and related accessories.

When someone offers something up for rent over a more extended period, we call such an arrangement a lease. For instance, you could lease a car for a year or two.

There are many reasons why renting works and many other reasons why someone would choose to part with money for a chance to use an item, property, or service you own. A few of them include:

- **To enjoy tax benefits:** many rental expenses are tax-deductible.
- **To use something for a short time.** Chartering a plane to an executive business meeting is an ideal example.
- **To enjoy the experience without paying the full cost of owning something,** especially

something that may be expensive. An example of this is when someone hires a top-of-the-line luxury sports car like a Ferrari.

- **To avoid the burden of maintaining a property or product.** Cars, especially expensive cars, have high overheads. For instance, buying tires for a Bugatti Veyron will set you back $30,000-$42,000, with the tires needing changing every 2,500 miles. Few people can afford such expensive maintenance, which makes leasing or renting a viable, reasonable choice.
- **When you don't have ready access to something, you may need to hire it.** For instance, if you are on vacation and you didn't bring your bicycle, you will need to hire one that you can ride.

Offering things or services up for rent is a high-potential income stream. Perhaps some things you currently own are idle and could earn you a regular income.

With a little insight and creativity, you can identify numerous things and opportunities that could provide you with rental income. In a later section, we shall explore a few rental income opportunities you could look into and exploit.

Distribution Systems

There's massive income potential in distribution, an area of businesses known as the marketing mix. A typical marketing mix consists of product, pricing, promotion, and distribution.

Distribution is highly valuable because no matter how great a product is, it is of no value if it can't reach the intended target audience. To capitalize on this business opportunity, the role you need to play is helping to bridge that need by making a product available to end consumers.

In a lot of ways, being a distributor makes you a marketer of products and services, which is ideal because, as a distributor, all you have to do is find a great product that sells well and then make it available to its potential market. You don't have to produce the product, or even come up with an original idea. You can leave such headaches to the manufacturer, producer, or inventor. All you have to do is create an effective distribution channel.

Moreover, with this income source, should a certain line of products become obsolete and therefore non-profitable, you can always jump-ship with ease and move to something else. The low risk and flexibility make distribution an attractive source of income.

However, you need to understand that distribution isn't just about taking someone else's hard work and taking advantage of it. The business model is vital for many reasons, a few of which are:

- **Value addition:** Distributors can use different means to add value to the product they are offering for sale. For instance, if you are a distributor of mobile phones, you can provide product manuals, demonstrate product features, or offer customer service.
- **Marketing:** As a distributor, to earn revenue from your business, you may take it upon yourself to launch marketing campaigns that help you move more products—leading to more sales, aka more profits in your pockets.
- **Quantity adjustment:** In some instances, the end-user may not be willing to purchase a product in bulk. In this case, as a distributor, you re-package the product in smaller quantities as a way of giving buyers convenience.
- **Reduced cost:** It would take a producer a lot of money to set up operations in every jurisdiction, thereby reaching a bigger audience. By relying on distributors, product manufacturers can save a lot of money—and hassle.

As you can see, besides being a profitable business model, distribution also adds a lot of value to the value chain.

The remarkable thing is that distribution can take on many forms. For instance, you can be a retailer who has a store that sells goods from suppliers at a profit. You can also be an agent who sells a product or a service at a commission or a wholesaler who sells to other retailers.

The beauty of today's world is that distribution can take on a digital form. For instance, if you start a blog that reviews electronics, your content essentially targets the electronics market. In this instance, you would build an audience of qualified prospects, which makes you an invaluable cog in the value chain process. Let's push this envelope a bit further:

Let's assume that after creating a database of prospects —perhaps an email list—you then decide to sell electronics to your list of targets.

In this case, you don't take on inventory; all you have to do is use affiliate links to redirect your prospects to a site owned by a major supplier. Whenever someone uses your affiliate link, the supplier fulfills the order—if you have a drop shipping agreement in place—and you collect a commission, a percentage of every sale made.

The distribution business system is an operation that you can run from practically anywhere in the world, with very few resources, all the while offering an extensive range of products and services.

Freelancing Systems

Would you like to start a business that has little overhead or inventory? A business you can run from a home office or the bedroom? A business that would not require a lot of startup capital?

If the answer to all of the above and related questions is yes, then you might want to try freelancing.

A freelancer is a businessperson who sells his or her services without any formal ties to a particular employer. Thus, as a freelancer, the main thing you will sell is your skill.

If you equip yourself with a valuable skill that allows you to provide a service that's in great demand and low supply, you'll find clients and likely never run out of work.

For instance, you might become a freelance web developer, software engineer, IT expert, statistician, video game developer, lawyer, graphic designer, writer, musician, artist, and so on. In other words, most of the people who become freelancers are self-employed professionals, many of whom are in the creative category.

In case you're wondering why you should consider becoming a freelancer, perhaps because you'd like to have a consistent paycheck, consider this:

Yes, freelancing is not the magic bullet, but certain advantages make it worthwhile. Here are some of these upsides:

- **You have time/schedule freedom:** Yes, unlike regular jobs where your employer sets your work hours for you, as a freelancer, you get the freedom to choose when to work, when to take a nap, when to watch TV, when to go on vacation, and when to stop taking on new assignments. Which 9-5 job can give you that kind of personal freedom?
- **You have control over your destiny:** Yes, as a freelancer, you determine how hard you'll work, how much you want to earn, fees you would like to charge, how fast you will keep advancing your expertise, and other such career factors.
- **You can exercise creative expression:** It's almost impossible to express creative ideas in an office environment where your boss dictates the dimensions of your work. That deficiency can be a very frustrating experience for a creative professional who feels that the ideas he or she brings to the table are concrete. As a

freelancer, you can talk it out with your clients, many of whom are usually open to new and fresh ideas.
- **You can make some money on the side:** You don't have to go all out and pursue a freelancing career path. You can hold down a 9-5 job while at the same time completing freelance projects on the side to supplement your income or to save for retirement.
- **It's a much better option:** Freelancing is better than any job because it provides a way to hedge your risk. If a day comes when you suddenly lose your job or something happens—like the coronavirus—and your boss has to cut your salary in half, you will have the option to pursue freelancing full-time, knowing that you're now well-established and could demand higher rates.

In case you're also wondering why businesses hire freelancers, there're a couple of reasons. For instance:

- **Quality of work:** Usually, freelancers who command top-dollar are at the very top of their fields, with vast experience under their belt. Because of this, someone seeking quality service always gets value for money.
- **Ease of interaction:** It's often difficult for

clients to request changes to assignments when they are dealing with major corporations that have a lot of bureaucracy. That's usually not the case with freelancers.

- **Freelancers may be cheaper overall:** Put yourself in the shoes of a typical businessman. For you, saving money and practicing efficient asset allocation is essential. What if you want a service like book-keeping, which is a one-time service. Should you hire a full-time accountant? That doesn't make sound business sense and is ineffective. On the other hand, calling a project-based freelancer whenever you need your books reconciled—probably once a month—makes economic sense.
- **Less management headache:** If a freelancer has established him or herself as a consummate professional, you can readily assume that he or she appreciates the importance of self-management. In contrast, employees usually shun their responsibilities and are often the worst at self-regulations—that's why many businesses restrict the use of social media during work hours. Having to oversee small tasks is a major drag that most business owners would rather avoid, which is why many of them now opt to hire freelancers.
- **Less risk:** It's risky to hire employees, especially

in today's business environment. What if you get stuck with unionized employees? What if you have no choice but to send them on paid leaves, create pensions schemes, as well as offer a "favorable working environment?"

Moreover, most business owners know that competitors are outsourcing work to top freelancers from around the world who demand less pay and don't come with all the excess baggage of in-house employees. To remain competitive—lest they file for chapter 11—they have to follow suit.

Aptitude Systems

You can also run a profitable business as a marketer of talent, or, if you are talented yourself, you can sell your talents.

Aptitude refers to an innate ability to perform specific tasks without developmental training. Training may certainly enhance performance, but with aptitude, the natural ability counts for much of the output. In other words, aptitude is another word for "innate talent."

Do you possess a talent that few people have? If so, then you could sell that talent and make a lot of money from it. However, if you don't possess natural inborn talents that can earn you a lot of money, you can manage and sell the talents of other people.

Although the notion might sound ridiculous, often, a lot of very talented people know more about their craft than how to find work and make money. It takes someone with connections and marketing expertise to bring out the best in these people. If you can become that person, you will be a blessing to these people and shall get handsomely rewarded for your efforts.

To drive my point, we'll look at an example from the football business. A player like Christiano Ronaldo is a phenomenally talented and dedicated player. However, every likelihood is that he knows very little about the football business and would struggle to succeed by himself.

To hedge against this, he seeks shelter under a capable talent management team. This team also helps him find work and negotiates his deals. Christiano, then, only has to concentrate on becoming a better soccer player by the day. It's an efficient operation, and both he and his team make money.

Aptitude systems work the same way in other dimensions. For instance, top musicians, actors, fashionistas, and other talented professionals have management teams that handle the business aspect of talent management.

Websites like Freelancer.com, Upwork.com, Fiverr.com, 99designs, and others play a similar role. They help top talent find their ideal audience of people willing to pay them for their work. By acting as a professional match-making service, these platforms make money. You can play such a role too and earn a decent profit without being a top talent yourself.

Passive Income Systems

Lastly, but not least, there are passive income systems.

A passive income is any income you earn from doing little or no active work. Most genuinely wealthy people have multiple passive income streams, and if you want to become personally wealthy, then you have to create multiple passive income streams as well.

If you always count on the money you earn from your primary vocation, your chances of ending up wealthy are slim—to none—because wealth is a result of having your money working for you. Passive investment avenues are the key to achieving that goal.

I need to point out something vitally important here:

Don't mistake a passive income for easy money because it's anything but that. In most cases, you should not consider a passive income as your primary source of income or wealth. Also, it takes upfront work, time, energy, and monetary investment to establish passive income streams. Additionally, no income stream is entirely passive: you will still need to put in some maintenance work to keep your passive investments performing optimally.

Unfortunately, this truth is not something you're likely to hear from "gurus" who want to sell you their passive income ideas. Most of the people who market passive income ideas dangle the prospect of get-rich-quick schemes that will continue making money on autopilot, without any work whatsoever. That is rarely the case.

In all my years in business, here's what I have learned about passive incomes:

You need to work hard and earn money from your primary vocation or business, and then invest your money in vehicles that can generate a passive income. That is the secret to earning income passively.

Over time, the money from your passive investments may grow to the point of taking care of all your basic needs, plus a few luxuries, but often, it takes years to get there. If you have the patience and the willingness to remain committed to the prospect, you'll eventually get there.

The basic message I'd like you to take away from this is that a passive income doesn't happen overnight, and many of the so-called passive investment ideas that bear fruits rapidly often demand a lot of upfront time, effort, and resources before you can reap the rewards of your hard work. By the time the paycheck lands in your pocket, you are not likely to agree with the passive income assessment.

That said, I'd like to list just a few passive income ideas at this point; we'll discuss them later. They include:

- Dividend income from stock investments
- Interest earned from a loan portfolio
- Interest earned from stock market investments
- Royalties from book sales
- Income from businesses where your active participation isn't necessary
- Rental income
- Income from real estate investment trusts (REITs)
- Interest from Certificates of Deposit
- Interests earned from bond investments

Now that you have the bigger picture in mind, in the next section, we will delve deeper into income opportunities that currently exist in the categories we have talked about so far:

45 ALTERNATIVE INCOME SOURCES

"Your economic security does not lie in your job; it lies in your power to produce – to think, to learn, to create, to adapt. True financial independence is not having wealth; it's having the power to produce wealth."

— STEPHEN .R. COVEY

This section will delve deeper into available opportunities within the categories we have discussed so far and that you can use to generate wealth.

My aim is that by the end of this section, you will be in a position to choose an idea or two that appeals to your abilities and aptitudes and that you can run with or work on as you get on your journey to financial security.

Let's get started:

Technology-Based Streams

At this point, you are well aware of the vast potential that exists in the technology sector, and the vast demand for technology products and services both for consumers and businesses.

If you are interested in this area, here are income-generating systems you can use to get started:

Website development and design

In the current digital world, almost every business imaginable needs to establish an online presence of some sort. Even though a business may not be conducting operations over the web, a website can act as a way to showcase a portfolio as a way to attract potential partners or business prospects.

In other words, in the current world, a website serves pretty much the same purpose as a traditional business card—and you know how important a business card can be—a fact that has increased the demand for people who can develop and design websites is high.

One thing you need to understand is that there's a slight difference between being a website designer and a developer. A designer creates a mockup of the website interface, the core concept.

This mockup gives an idea of how the website will look after its creation. The idea behind this is similar to how car manufacturers create a model before building a car or how architects create housing designs and miniature models for illustration purposes.

On the other hand, a website developer does the actual work of building the website. He (or she) brings the concept to life by coding or programming all the visual elements and functionalities illustrated by the model created by the designer. If it's at all possible for you, it's best to possess both skills since few people are willing to hire a designer and developer separately.

If web development interests you, you'll be happy to know that Udemy has several related courses, and you can also find free web tutorials that will equip you with the skills you need to have to take on this kind of work.

Software design and development

Along the same lines as websites, we have computer software design and development.

The current nature of the business world has necessitated the need for intuitive computer software that can take care of or streamline various business functions.

For instance, a business may need computer software with which to perform its accounting, to manage its human resources, keep records, process payments, create receipts, manage customer orders as well as requests, manage communications around the workplace, and so much more.

Many of these functions are unique, which means businesses require custom software solutions instead of off-the-shelf software. These market conditions have raised the demand for software development and design expertise.

If you are technically inclined and are passionate about software development, you can become a freelance software developer who gets hired to create software solutions.

The good thing about software development is that software developers get paid well because of the technical nature of the work. According to Indeed.com, software developers can earn upwards of $100,000 a year.

Another good thing is that you don't need a degree in computer science to become a software developer. You can self-teach yourself this skill by reading the countless books on the topic and working through tutorials and digital courses that can equip you with the requisite skills. All you need is the passion, the patience to learn, and the willingness to succeed.

Programming

You can also earn a decent living as a freelance programmer, which is a subset of software development.

Programmers complete the software development process by coding software components, especially with large scale projects.

You see, software projects can vary in terms of size and complexity. In certain circumstances, as a software developer, your role might be to build a simple system, such as a customer service portal, which is work you can complete individually.

In other instances, a project can be remarkably big and complex. Take the example of accounting software such as QuickBooks, which is versatile and multi-faceted.

Creating such an ambitious software has many moving cogs that require teamwork and consultation.

Often, such software programs bring onboard programmers with various skillsets and levels of experience to code specific components of such a project. With that comes the opportunity to become a freelance programmer. As you read this, there is a software project going on that will demand skills and specialty in a particular area, and the person to fill that role might be you.

To get started, select a programming language you feel drawn to and strive to become extremely good at it; if you do, there's no doubt in my mind that you won't struggle too much to find work.

Java is one of the best programming languages to learn because of its vast usage in the programming industry. Other programming languages you can learn are C, C#, C++, Ruby on Rails, Python, Perl, PHP, JavaScript, Visual Basic, and others.

Because of the complexity involved, few people have a genuine interest in becoming programmers, which means if you master a language and become a reasonably good expert in that field, there is less competition, and the projects pay well too.

App development

Since the advent of smartphones, many people have discovered the massive income potential heralded by these handheld devices.

Smartphones are small computers that can carry out a wide variety of useful tasks. The potential here is so substantive that as of this writing, much of it remains untapped.

Moreover, because businesses want apps that streamline workplace processes, and the general population wants innovative app-based solutions to common challenges, the demand for app developers is high—and promises to continue being high long into the foreseeable future.

There's also a high demand for apps from educational institutions that want to make learning an interactive and fun experience. Wall Street is also clamoring for apps that will give investors the ability to execute trades from anywhere in the world.

Additionally, various startups are looking for innovative programmers who can create apps that help them claim a share of the exploding app market.

Even the health industry is demanding apps. This morning, I used an app on my iPhone to measure my heart rate, all by placing my finger-tip on the camera.

Some apps help people measure their walking distance, stay fit by recommending workouts, and so on.

With new technologies popping up almost every other day—like facial recognition, voice recognition, artificial intelligence, virtual reality, augmented reality, machine learning, and so on—the demand for apps isn't going to decrease any time soon.

Overall, now is the best time to become an app developer, and thanks to their uptake by the general populace, rest assured that some business or visionary out there is looking for a capable app developer who can bring an app idea to life.

Because app development is a subset of software engineering, if you have a passion for coding, you can become a well-paid app developer. The standout thing about app development is that today, getting started is easier than it used to be a couple of years ago, thanks to kits and frameworks that make app development a breeze.

In 2014, I used a kit from Oracle Apex to build an app. I remember that it had prebuilt modules that I just reused and that I didn't even have to write a single line of code. I have not been in the app development world for years, but I am fairly certain that things are much better today than they were back then.

SEO

SEO stands for search engine optimization, which is an area of digital marketing that is in high demand, and that tends to pay SEO professionals very well and for a good reason.

You see:

Today, most of us use search engines to seek information or research products to buy. We even use search engines to navigate the web and visit our favorite sites.

For instance, when I want to visit Facebook, I don't open up my browser and type www.facebook.com. Instead, I open Google and type Facebook. Then I click on the first result.

Thus, search engines are a key source of traffic for anyone who has an online presence, with high, organic traffic translating into more business revenue. Because of this, businesses are always willing to pay someone with the skillset to optimize web pages and content for search engines.

SEO usually involves writing website content—a skill called SEO copywriting—that features strategically placed keywords that searchers typically use when looking for answers on sites like Google

SEO also involves other things like making sure a website has clean code and formatted in a way that makes it easy for search engine spiders to crawl the site. It may also involve linking the website to other authoritative sites in the same niche.

Most people who run websites don't have the necessary SEO skills and are thus always willing to pay someone to take care of these details for them, usually at a fair fee—Neil Patel is a standout example of the income potential in SEO

Domain name broker

Domain names are a must-have for anyone who wants to have a website on the internet.

A domain name is what internet users type into their browser tabs so that they can navigate to your website and do business with you. For instance, www.google.com is a domain name. A special computer translates the name to an IP address that then points to a server that hosts the website.

To acquire a domain name, you have to buy it. The money usually goes to an organization called the Internet Corporation for Assigned Names and Numbers (ICANN) in the U.S. Governments around the world also pocket the gains from country-specific domains such as .au, .us, .ca, .uk, and so on.

Here, the opportunity lies in the fact that you can help register a domain on behalf of someone and pocket some profit in the process. That is, you can become a domain name broker representing the ICANN or a local government. In essence, you become a lead generating machine.

We have already talked about how valuable websites are to every business existing on the planet; many people are also waking up to this realization. For instance, Tech giant Verisign once reported that the domain names registered per day are more than 144,000.

With that many people registering new domains every day, you have the chance to get a piece of the game; you only need to open a domain registrar agency or operation.

If you are a programmer, you can design websites for this kind of thing, or, if not, you could hire someone to do it for you. Once you have a website that allows people to look up and register their domain names, you can market your business in all sorts of ways and join the game.

Google Ads

Internet marketing is one of the most profitable business opportunities available today because every business on the web needs marketing to generate revenue.

While organic search traffic is free, it typically takes a lot of time before a website—or a page on a website—

can show up on the first or second page of Google. The pages that get the most organic traffic are the ones on the first and second pages of the search engine results page (SERP) because most people don't go beyond the second page.

What should this tell you? It should tell you that SEO is not for everyone. It's remarkably competitive, especially in popular niches.

That makes paid advertising the most viable option for those willing to spend some money to tip the odds of the traffic game in their favor. In this regard, Google Ads delivers good results.

Google owns the most expansive advertisement real estate on the web. They have partner sites, the search engine itself, Gmail, YouTube, and every other site that's part of Alphabet Inc. Google also has the most accurate data about people who browse the web. Facebook is a close second.

Together, they have capable ad platforms that make it easy to create targeted ads based on demographics and characteristics, thereby allowing businesses to reach a well-defined audience. For these reasons alone, Ads are a must-do for anyone hoping to run ads on the web for business purposes.

Paid ads, however, require expertise; otherwise, it's possible to spend thousands of dollars on ads that have zero return on investment to show for it.

Thus, if you have paid ads expertise, businesses will down your doors, asking you to run ads that can offer great ROI, and you can charge mighty big bucks for your knowledge.

Cybersecurity expert

Tech-based innovations have opened up new and endless opportunities for criminals in cyberspace, mainly because most of these innovations don't have security as their base DNA.

For instance, in the early days—pre-2010—of what we now call web 2.0, eCommerce websites were popular, but they had fundamental flaws. For example, many of these sites had insufficient security checks at high-value components like databases and user input interfaces.

Thus, with a bit of technical know-how, it was fairly easy to manipulate these websites to give up private information stored in the database—like usernames, passwords, Credit Card Numbers, and so on.

Another possibility was to trick the website into making expensive purchases at steep discounts, zero costs, or even negative costs. These were the harsh realities of security holes caused by advancing technology. Today, we are at a much more "safer" place.

Cybersecurity professionals have plugged many of those holes, but new ones keep popping up, and as long as we keep innovating, new computer vulnerabilities will keep coming to the fore; it's a game that never ends.

You can build a successful career out of finding and fixing security holes in computer systems, which, besides being fun, is also richly rewarding.

Glassdoor estimates that cyber Security Experts earn an estimated $100,000 every year. Currently, various reputable organizations are offering many free and paid cybersecurity courses at affordable costs. CompTIA, Offensive Security, and Cybrary are ideal places to start. Countless good books also exist on the subject. The only investment needed is your time, effort, and passion for the subject.

Content-Based Streams

Let's explore content-based ideas you can use to generate income:

Blogging

If you love writing, blogging is the first option you should consider.

A blog is a website where you post written material consistently, with the content written in a relaxed, conversational tone instead of a formal one. Think of a blog as some sort of digital diary.

Another typical characteristic of blogs is that the posted content appears displayed in reverse chronological order, with the most recent post displayed first for readers to see and older posts archived.

Successful blogs you may be familiar with include Gizmodo, Lifehacker, TechCrunch, and Mashable.

When starting a blog, the goal is to establish a list of loyal readers who actively interact with your content. Once you have that in place, you can monetize that audience by offering paid products such as eBooks, courses, consultancy services, affiliate product offerings, etc. This way, you can make a good living even with a medium-sized audience.

Brian Clark of Copyblogger media is an excellent example of how blogging can turn into a very successful venture. He started the CopyBlogger blog in 2006 as a means through which he could share great content around the subject—copywriting—and using content as a marketing tool instead of harpooning prospects with direct marketing sales pitches.

True to his message, he never spent a dollar on advertising his blog. All his traffic was "organic." Yet, Copy-

Blogger is currently one of the top blogs on the web, and Brian Clark nets an average of $10 million a year. His success has been so inspirational that Forbes did a feature on him.

If you would like to follow his footsteps, pick a niche topic you are passionate about, and then get down to the business of creating great content that resonates with your audience. From there, the only way is up.

There is no shortage of online resources that can help you start a blog. Quicksprout's resource, a blog run by Neil Patel, is especially good.

On-demand courses

The competitiveness of the modern business environment has caused many people to embrace upgrading their skills through self-learning.

What most people are now realizing is that a college education is not what it used to be because most of the material taught in academic circles is impractical in the modern business world.

Additionally, a college education is abhorrently expensive. As I write this, the overall student loan burden in America alone stands at a staggering $1.6 billion, a tragic situation indeed.

For these reasons—and many others—more and more people are finding value in self-teaching through on-demand courses sold on the web. Most of these courses are cheap, well-designed, up-to-date, and usually created to teach specialized topics. In other words, on-demand courses offer great value for money.

Today, you can find a course on any subject you can imagine, which is a great income opportunity. If you are an expert at anything someone may wish to learn, you can generate thousands of dollars from designing and selling an on-demand course to an ideal audience. You can start on Udemy.

To get started, conduct market research by looking at Udemy data on which video courses are selling best and then create and launch a class that meets market needs. Plus, the platform offers tutorials and step-by-step guides detailing how to prepare high-quality course material for sale.

When Walter, a 25-year-old computer zealot profiled by Entrepreneur magazine in 2014, came across Udemy by chance, he quickly decided to learn what it takes to publish on the platform. He then proceeded to design a mini-course on creating an iPhone app for beginners. He offered the course at a measly $29 to attract buyers but then adjusted the price to $199. He went on to earn $66,533 within a month.

Years have passed, and countless people have had enormous success selling on Udemy and other on-demand course platforms. Some have grossed hundreds of thousands of dollars; others have grossed millions in course sales.

Book publishing

Perhaps you have always wanted to become a published author, but the prospect of having to pitch publishing agents and houses, only to receive countless, disheartening rejections has always held you back.

If you can relate, here's some good news:

Technology has disrupted the publishing business. Today, you can become a self-published author at the click of a button and make a lot of money in the process.

You can start this venture by publishing eBooks, which are books published in digital format so that readers can read through a device such as a smartphone, a PC, a tablet, a laptop, and so on.

All you have to do is choose a topic, write the book, have a professional proof-read, edit, and format it accordingly, create a cover—or hire someone to create one—and then once the book is ready, publish it on a digital marketplace such as Amazon Kindle Store. Once you have done that, all you have to do is market the book so that you can attract sales.

EBook publishing is an especially great idea if you already have an audience that is enthusiastic about your content. That's why it's best to start a blog before you write an eBook. This way, you can test your ideas and find out what issues your audience is facing based on their feedback. Then, when you publish, your success is nothing short of a guarantee because all you have to do is serve the book to your audience.

Seth Godin is an outstanding example of the potential in book publishing. Today, he is a well-known internet marketer who has published lots of marketing ideas on his blog, Sethgodin.com, which has a very engaged audience. Because of having an engaged audience, most of the books he's published have gone on to become bestsellers, primarily because he sold to his blog readers first.

There are lots of other success stories of writers earning small fortunes from self-publishing eBooks. Nothing's stopping you from joining this bandwagon.

Copywriting

You can also make good money as a copywriter, which is writing meant to offer a product or service for sale

If you can write well enough to move 1 or 2 (out of 100) readers to make a purchase, then you can become a well-paid copywriter, especially if you can create content that moves audiences and triggers them to take the desired action, which is how you make money.

As a result, copywriters are some of the highest-paid professionals. Many earn six figures a year, with exceptional ones making seven, and even eight figures a year.

In case you're wondering why a business would pay someone so much money, it's simple:

Businesses will pay top dollar for a skilled copywriter who writes winning copy because such copy can generate millions of dollars revenue in sales, especially if presented to a broad-enough audience. In this business, money is the key motivator for writers and their clients.

In the old days, direct mailing was the most common type of copywriting. A company would copy write a newsletter that it would then deliver through the mail, asking prospects to buy a particular product or service. If a pitch moved a prospect, the next step was to place an order, also via mail.

Although that system is old, even today, direct mailing still generates a significant number of sales—that's why you get junk mail—, with copywriters who write those solicitations receiving handsome remuneration.

Fortunately, you don't have to direct-mail people brochures. Today, the internet is the new conduit for product and service solicitations, and copywriting is a skill whose demand is still high.

The opportunity is even bigger now because today, we can use various means and channels to deliver sales copy. For instance, businesses can deliver sales copy via email, social media, blog posts, press releases, advertorials, Google Ads, white papers, and so on. Because of the proliferation of all these new channels, the opportunity to become a well-paid copywriter has more than doubled over the past few years.

You see, each of these channels demands a unique style of effective copywriting. That means you can establish yourself as a specialist in any one of these areas.

Copywriting is a precise art that will require study and practice, yes, but in the long-run, it's pay off for whoever is willing to work at it is handsome. If you are interested, start by reading the book The Copywriter's Handbook by Robert W. Bly, someone many seasoned copywriters consider one of the top copywriters in America today.

You don't have to stop at producing written content, especially if you don't have a passion for it. Audio content is also very popular today, and you can use it to build a substantial following.

Podcasting

If you've never heard of it, a podcast is just audio-based content made available to a subscriber-base for download, usually as a series.

The model is pretty much the same as blogging: you create engaging content, and when your audience is big enough, you monetize it, which is precisely what John Lee Dumas of Entrepreneur on Fire has done.

His podcast, which focuses on delivering inspirational messages to aspiring entrepreneurs, is one of the most popular today. I can't estimate how many subscribers the podcast has, but his influence is far-reaching, so much so that Mr. Dumas earns millions of dollars each year. Back in 2014, Forbes profiled him and reported his income as being roughly $2 million a year.

If you're wondering how he makes money from podcasting, for one thing, he coaches students and offers some of his content on a premium basis.

Now, I am sure that if you created a podcast that generated even a tenth of that income, you would be financially content and free, right? If so, then you might wish to get started. If he can do it, so can you.

YouTube has plenty of Podcasting tutorials for beginners; you can also buy related, on-demand courses:

YouTube

The demand for video content has exploded over the last few years, and according to Clickz, by 2022, 82% of traffic on the web will be to video content. That means the opportunity for video content is enormous, and you can take advantage of it to generate an income by becoming a YouTube creator.

According to a 2019 report from Statista, YouTube is the biggest video content provider in the world. Services like Netflix, Hulu, and Amazon Prime lag behind it.

Worth noting is that with video content, we are playing the same old content game: all you have to do is post great content, build, and then monetize an audience. The content can take on many different styles.

Take the example of Ray William Johnson. He started his YouTube channel, *"Equals Three,"* in 2009, with a primary focus on posting satirical reviews of viral videos.

His content was so good, and because it resonated with a lot of people, he became very popular and was among the first people to rake up 5 million subscribers. He once reported that some of the content on his channel received more views than mainstream television. Since then, Ray William Johnson has gone on to be in over five movies and TV shows. His net worth stands at a staggering $18.2 million.

Many other content creators have achieved varying levels of success in different niches and through monetizing their YouTube channels in different ways.

If you wish to start a YouTube channel, start by reading this guide first. Additionally, seek guidance from people who have done well in it before. For instance, you can take a Udemy course that teaches you everything you need to do from start to finish.

Social media influencer

You can also make a living as a social media influencer. An influencer is a public figure who holds a great deal of influence over a large group of people. When the medium is social media, the title becomes "social media influencer." In other words, if you have a large enough social audience that resonates with your content, you are a social media influencer.

As an influencer, you are in a position of power because people can pay you to drive all sorts of agendas. Most of the time, people in business will pay you to promote products and services to your audience, something Huda Kattan has managed to do so well.

She began as a blogger, posting makeup tutorials. She got her big break when she moved to Instagram, a platform mainly driven by high-quality visual content.

Today, she boasts a following of 47.4 million followers, one of the highest in her niche. She has managed to start a company, Huda Beauty, where she is the CEO. She sells all sorts of beauty products, many of which celebrities patronize, and Forbes estimates her current net worth to be $610 million.

Her example is extreme, and most people will never attain her level of wealth, but the point here is that the opportunity is there and substantial enough to warrant your attention. I know of many minor league influencers who are earning high to low six figures. Instagram holds great promise for most people.

Distribution Streams

Opportunities also exist in distribution. Here are a few of them:

ECommerce

Do you wish to run a store that has little overhead? Do you want to start a business that will not involve the burden of rent, and that you can operate your basement? If that's the case, then you might consider starting an eCommerce store— an online shop.

If you pick a popular niche where products are in high demand and the competition is low, your e-store will do very well, especially considering that most consumers are currently shopping online.

According to statistical data presented by Optinmonster, roughly 69% of Americans have completed an online shopping transaction. Moreover, estimates show that global online sales will gross $4 trillion this year. Additional data reveals that by 2023 roughly 91% of the entire U.S population will be doing their shopping online.

In other words, now is the best time to start an eCommerce store, and if you do your due diligence, you can position yourself as a major online retailer in the future.

All you have to do is find a supplier who is struggling to move a product and who is in a potentially lucrative niche. That supplier will be more than happy to work with you to move more products. That's how most retail operations run.

Do you suppose that a superstore like Walmart or Amazon purchases all their stock in cash? No! Most of their stock is from suppliers who wish to present their products to the market. The same case applies to an online store.

The internet has an unlimited number of resources that can take you by the hand and show you how to start an online store. A simple Google search is all it takes to get started.

Affiliate marketing

Affiliate marketing is another lucrative way of doing business online without putting too much of your resources on the line.

Becoming an affiliate marketer is comparable to being a salesperson in the sense that in both, you pitch a product or service. Once a target audience buys into what you are selling, you collect commissions on every sale made. The primary difference between the two is that affiliate marketing operates online, and you make a sale by providing an affiliate link that connects your target audience to the product or service up for sale.

Affiliate marketing is one of the most lucrative distribution models, especially if you know how to create content that resonates with a broad audience—as you can see, we're back to content marketing; it's because online, content is everything.

Affiliate marketing is one of the most effective, low-risk methods of monetizing a particular audience. It makes it possible to generate income without ever taking the risk to create a product or service of your own.

Before you start creating content, conduct research so that you can choose a low-lying fruit niche where you can affiliate yourself with various products and services from which you can net a tidy profit from each successful referral.

Once you nail down your niche, start creating content. The content you create can be in any form you want. You can start a podcast, a blog, an Instagram page, or a YouTube channel.

I can go on and on about how great affiliate marketing is, but if you want step by step details that includes real-world case studies, you will immensely enjoy reading this post created by Neil Patel.

Network marketing

Are you a charismatic person with a real passion for selling? Do you have an easy way with people? If yes, you should also look into network marketing, which works as follows:

You sign up with a company that sells quality, highly-demanded products. From there, your job is to generate sales and recruit a team that does the same.

Your income will mainly come from the sales of the products you pitch prospects, but you will also earn a small percentage of the sales made by the team members you recruit under you. Since your team—if well trained and up to the task—may generate more sales than you do, if you have a large enough team, you can generate a reasonably high income.

You can pursue network marketing both online as well as offline. If you are the stay-at-home type, then you will prefer working with a network marketing company that conducts business online.

When considering this business model, it's best to be highly aware because of the various pyramid schemes masquerading as legitimate network marketing companies.

These companies make money by advising you to "buy your opportunity into the company," usually by offering starter kits. Some, additionally, sell dangerous products or ones designed to rip off people.

With such companies, it's common to discover that the top network marketers within the business make most of their money from recruiting new people instead of sales generated by selling products to the public.

Before venturing into network marketing with any company, conduct research, and do your due diligence, lest you join a pyramid scheme masquerading as a legitimate network marketing company.

Here is a list of some reputable network marketing companies:

- Neolife International
- Amway
- Forever Living Products
- Avon
- Oriflame
- Herbalife Nutrition
- Legal Shield
- Organo Gold

Digital marketing

With a lot of business conducted online these days, social media platforms are becoming the preferred way for businesses to generate sales and leads, which is great, but:

Most well-established businesses started in the era of traditional marketing media such as print, radio, and television. Thus, while these businesses are well-versed in the art of traditional marketing, many are slow to adapt to and embrace the emerging world of digital marketing.

Many are struggling, spending thousands, sometimes millions of advertising dollars on digital marketing strategies that don't work in the modern world. You can help correct this by offering your digital marketing expertise and offering to handle a business's marketing needs in the social media space.

Digital marketing is an incredibly potent income idea because businesses allocate millions of dollars to their marketing budgets —since it's a key generator of revenue—,which means if you have provable digital marketing expertise, you'll earn an eye-popping income.

To get started with this business model, all you have to do is acquire the necessary marketing skills and stay current on the latest techniques; if you do that, your skills will be in high demand.

Various platforms can equip you with digital marketing skills. Ryan Deiss's platform, DigitalMarketer.com, is one of the foremost authorities on the subject of digital marketing.

Franchising

A franchise is a business arrangement where one party grants another the legal rights to use its processes, name, and logo to sell products and services.

As you know, it takes time and a lot of effort to build a business brand that has a positive reputation. Franchising allows you to leverage the goodwill created by an already-established brand. Under the right circumstances, a franchise is less risky than starting a business from scratch.

After seeing how successful franchises like KFC, Subway, Domino's, Burger King, and McDonald's have operated, you might want to start such a business, but on a smaller, less-global scale.

As a franchisee, you pay an upfront fee, plus agree to pay a portion of your profits to the franchisor. If you keep these two things in mind before you get started and are okay with them, then franchising is a practical way to start a business.

Drop-shipping

If you have little money and no extra space, but you want to start an online business that involves selling a particular class of products that excites you, then drop-shipping is the best way to accomplish that.

Drop-shipping involves setting up an e-store where you list products and take orders from customers but keep no inventory. Instead, you liaise with the manufacturer or some third party who warehouses the stock and fulfills customer orders. Your role is to market the products and take orders.

Although drop shipping sounds a lot like affiliate marketing, there a few key differences between the two models, one of which has to do with pricing. For instance, as an operator of a drop-shipping business, you alone decide the retail price of the item you are selling, a luxury you don't get with affiliate marketing.

Overall, drop-shipping is a sound approach for those who have minimal resources but who still want to start an eCommerce store.

Shopify provides a service that makes it easier for people who have little or no technical background to manage the intricacies of operating a drop-shipping operation.

Rental Streams

If you have an appetite for rental income streams, consider the following avenues:

Real estate

Human beings need places in which to reside, and businesses need premises from which to operate. These two realities guarantee the continued demand for real estate. That's why over 90% of millionaires own real estate, thereby making the opportunity as logical as putting on socks before shoes, which further highlights the fact that you don't have to need unusual business insights to make money. Some opportunities are staring at you.

Worth noting is that getting started in real estate isn't for everyone because getting in demands a considerable, upfront financial commitment irrespective of where you want to purchase commercial or residential real estate.

To circumvent this, real estate investors usually start in some other area of business where they can make money before they set their eyes on the real estate industry.

Just as technology has revolutionized many other areas of life, it has also changed how much money you need to invest in the real estate market. Today, the cost of investing in the real estate market is low, more so if you invest in Real Estate Investment Trusts (REITs).

A REIT is a company that owns a portfolio of income-producing real estate, and that sells its shares to willing, outside investors. For this reason, it's best to assume that REITs are a form of capital investment, which we will discuss later in the passive income streams subsection.

Car rental services

You can turn your car into an asset by offering your car up for rent. In doing so, you will be earning a regular income every time someone leases your car. You may even find the business so profitable that you end up acquiring an entire fleet and starting a legally-established car rental business.

The great thing about this business is that you can run an online operation. All you have to do is get a talented programmer to design a website that allows prospects to book your fleet of vehicles online. From there, all you have to do is engage in digital marketing.

The potential here is like a bottomless pit, which is why companies like Rentalcars.com, USA Cars rental, and Carrentals.com have become major successes. You can test the concept with your car, and if the results impress you, you can then go all in.

Licensing

Licensing is simply the act of granting another party or parties the permission to do something, own something, or use something. For instance, the government issues business licenses. Every time a license expires, a business has to renew it, from which the government makes money.

You can patent a product, service, or idea, and then set out to make money from licensing it. Let's say you identify a new way of doing something, say, for example, a new, more efficient way of bottling wine or alcohol that is exciting and revolutionary. You could patent the idea and make a lot of money licensing it to all wine and alcohol producers.

To make good money from licensing, you must have a novel or revolutionary product, service, or idea. That means you have to conduct considerable research and come up with something that has that wow-factor—and that is also so beneficial that people would be willing to pay you to use it.

Leases

Leasing is very much similar to renting. The only difference is that leasing is longer and can go for a year or more. Renting, on the other hand, often implies a short-term arrangement such as the end of the month, week, or even day.

Properties such as vehicles, land, and buildings are the assets usually offered up for lease. Other items that can fit the leasing model are:

- intellectual-properties, such as computer programs
- Businesses,
- Industrial equipment
- Intangible assets (such as radio frequencies)

Usually, as a lessor or asset owner, you draw up a contractual agreement stipulating the terms the lessee must adhere to, the payment schedules, among other things.

Music and book royalties

If you would like to venture into creative works such as music and book authoring, you will be happy to know that you can sell your rights to a third party who can then compensate you regularly when your product generates sales.

Speaking of books:

Recent changes in the publishing sector have made the traditional path of selling your book to a publisher less attractive, primarily because self-publishing is easier — and sometimes more profitable. For instance, publishers often give authors 30% of book sales. Amazon pays 70% in royalties.

The main benefit of taking the traditional publishing route is that reputable publishers often pay authors a significant advance before the book hits the market, with royalties—albeit low—coming in later. Additionally, a book may end up selling more copies if a major publishing house endorses it.

Weigh your options and decide which path is best for you; the difference is a matter of strategy and preference. For instance, if many publishers reject your book, but you feel that it has great potential, you can self-publish it and then market it to your target audience.

Aptitude Streams

If you have a genuine talent or something you love, you can also make money with it. While there're many ways you can go about this, social media is one of the best ways to market your skills, abilities, and aptitude to the world.

We have discussed the potential in content marketing. Well, social media is a conduit for great content. You can establish a page or profile and post pictures or videos and attract a particular audience. Down the road, you can use all sorts of monetization strategies to generate income.

Here are some of the best aptitude-based income streams:

Creative art and painting

Do you like creating original art, graphic designs, or paintings? If you do, you could start a social media page where you showcase your work to millions of fans. Instagram is a particularly good fit for this because of the visual nature of the medium.

If you can't fathom the potential attached to this income stream, consider the following examples:

- Boo Simms
- Luke Choice

- Jessica Walsh
- Richard Mehl
- Tobias Hall

Music

The number of musicians who have social media to thank for their fame will surprise you. Examples include Justin Bieber, Cardi B, Shawn Mendes, Calvin Harris, The Weekend, The Chainsmokers, and Charlie Puth. If you're a musician, you can follow suit.

Comedy

If you can make people laugh, you can make a ton of money online because entertainment is one of the main reasons why people go online, especially social media. You could make short clips and post them on YouTube, Facebook, or Instagram. There's no doubt that however distinct your humor is, you'll find fans willing to support your venture.

You might recall Ray William Johnson, who, in 2011, quickly created an audience of 5 million from making funny videos, some of which are so popular that tons of people still watch them.

Other comedians who have social media to thank for their success are Mo Gillian, Brian Limond, Celeste Barber, Ilana Glazer, James Veitch, and Collen Ballinger.

Acting

If you are an actor who wishes to land a role in Hollywood or reality TV someday, social media could help you get started.

If you closely follow a story such as that of Bo Burnham, who became an overnight YouTube sensation at age 16 and later attracted the attention of Hollywood directors, you'll see what's possible here.

Make-up artistry

Women have an insatiable appetite for makeup tips, which is why Huda Kattan, CEO of Huda Beauty, is the person she is today. Even today, even though she is famous and the head of a very successful business, she still posts makeup tutorials and content on social media.

Fashion designing

Do you dream of becoming a fashionista or launching your own clothesline? Perhaps you dream of signing mega-deals with clothing lines such as Polo, Gucci, Nordstrom, and Armani.

Well, there're plenty of opportunities in this niche as well; Instagram alone can be incredibly impactful. Consider the following people:

- Chiara Ferragni

- Camila Coehlo
- Negin Mirsalehi
- Aimee Song
- Julie Sarinana

Photography

If you are a photographer, or you want to become a successful one, now is the best time to get started, thanks to the power of social media.

Think all those Instagram influencers who post crisp, sharp photos. Do you think they're the ones behind the camera? Rarely! Most hire the services of professional photographers, which makes this business model very viable.

Here are a few inspiring examples:

- Chris Burkard
- David Guttenfelder
- Pei Ketron
- Jimmy Chin
- Murad Osmann

Catering

Perhaps you're a skilled culinary master who would love to get hired for your talent. Here too, you can market yourself on social media and achieve tangible results.

All you have to do is take and share nice photos and videos with your audience using mediums such as YouTube and Instagram. You may impress people so much that they start asking you to publish your recipes, which means you can sell eBooks to them.

Here are a few examples:

- Bites and Bashes
- Contemporary Catering
- Your Platter Matters
- Modern Art Catering
- 24 Carrots Catering

Event planning

According to Entrepreneur Magazine, the event planning industry grosses roughly $500 billion annually. If you have your sight set on this niche, the chances are high that you'll achieve success.

Posting your work on social media is a great way to get the word out. For instance, look at these people who have managed to pull it off:

- Mindy Weiss
- Wink Design and Events

- International Event Company
- Little Miss Party
- Sasha Souza Events

PASSIVE INCOME STREAMS

If you would like to create passive income streams, here're ideas to get you started:

Dividend-paying investments

One of the soundest ways to earn a passive income is to invest in avenues that pay dividends. As mentioned earlier, a dividend is a portion of the profit from a business operation distributed among investors.

Some company stocks pay dividends to shareholders regularly, which means if you have money invested in a quality dividend paying stock, you can expect to receive passive income regularly. If the price of the stock increases, even better.

Another option here is investing in ETFs. An ETF is a fund that holds a collection of stocks in a particular sector. For instance, examples of ETFs in the technology sector are:

- Factset
- Technology Select Sector SPDR Fund
- Vanguard Information Technology ETF

- Direxion
- Global X Computing ETF

ETFs trade like ordinary stocks, which means you can buy and sell one from an exchange. When you do, you profit from the potential increase in price and also earn the right to a share of the profits the business generates.

ETFs are an ideal option because you don't have to pick individual stocks; you leave the job to experts. Additionally, it diversifies your risk since your portfolio will consist of holdings in various stocks, which mitigates risk should one company go out of business or experience significant price drops.

Laundromat business

A laundromat is a place where you can have your clothes cleaned and dried via coin-operated machine washers.

The machines do the work, which means the business needs little oversight, which is what makes this opportunity especially appealing to someone seeking a passive income opportunity. When conveniently located, a laundromat can generate above-average returns on investment with minimal supervision.

Consider the case of a couple, Mandy and Don Situ, who operate a laundromat in Queens. On their first day in business, they netted a measly $52, but by the end of the month, they had grossed well over $10,000. The enterprise has been enjoying stable growth ever since.

Vending machines

Coin-operated vending machines help dole out small items such as snacks, drinks, confectionaries, and so on. Like coin-operated washers, vending machines require minimal supervision, which means the income they generate qualifies as passive income.

Navdeep Tuteja owns and operates the site SVAvending.com. He is living proof that the vending machine business works. Inspired by the number of people spending time around vending machines during his days in employment, he started his first vending machine operation. His wife thought it was a gamble and didn't talk to him for a full week. Things went well for Navdeep.

In his first year, he earned a net return of $120% on his investment. He says he went from owning one vending machine to creating a business that operates 27 of them, with offices in three major cities. Today, he is looking to franchise his business, which is a smart idea.

You can read HealthyVending.com to find out all details related to starting a vending machine business.

Limited partnerships

A limited partnership is a business arrangement that involves at least one general partner, the person who oversees the entire operation and assumes most of the risk.

As a limited partner, you invest your money in the business and collect a share of profits proportional to your investment in the enterprise. Your liability in the business does not exceed your investment, which minimizes your risk is minimal.

Limited partnerships tend to work well in sectors like real estate, small business, professional practice, and the filming industry.

Peer to peer lending

Last but not least, you can make your money work for you and earn passive income in the lending business. In this case, you will be operating much like a bank, building a portfolio of loan assets, and generating interest on the principal.

You will be lending to parties like individuals and businesses who either want to avoid the hassle of borrowing from a financial institution or who simply can't qualify for such credit. Whatever the case, the interest you earn from this type of lending activity can outpace earnings from many other types of investments.

Platforms like LendingClub and Prosper make it easy to get started with this business model because they bring together lenders and borrowers and facilitate the lending-borrowing process.

Worth mentioning here is that to run such a venture profitably, you have to be good with numbers and able to minimize your risk by diversifying over a large number of borrowers.

Freelancing Systems

You can also generate income from freelancing. Here're some ideas to start you off:

Online gigs

Do you have an in-demand skill such as writing, graphic design, web design, computer programming, social media management, etc. that you would like to generate a steady income from by providing your service to a steady stream of clients?

If your answer to the above question is "yes," you should look into online freelance marketplaces, websites used by clients seeking competent professionals who can complete various tasks. By joining such a website, you can find clients who would be willing to pay well for your services.

To increase your chances of landing jobs, you need to create a professional-looking profile and portfolio that illustrates your skills, abilities, and experience. You also need to browse through the listings and pitch your expertise to potential hirers.

The more clients you pitch, the higher your chances of landing an assignment, especially if the hirer feels you've made your case well. Overall, gigs marketplaces are a numbers game where, if you pitch enough listings, you will eventually land a project. Depending on the number of listings on the particular marketplace you're using, you could land a project each day, week, or month.

Some platforms advertise the cost the client is willing to pay, while others give you the chance to negotiate your fees. The fees you charge will depend on your level of experience, how confident you feel about the value you provide, and your income goals.

The most stand out benefit of using these platforms is that you can establish relationships that can form the basis of long-term future assignments with clients. Once you have a client base that is stable enough to guarantee consistent income, you can exit these platforms and build your business in other ways.

Here's a list of gig websites you can use check:

- Freelancer.com
- Upwork
- Fiverr
- People Per Hour
- Guru.com
- DesignCrowd

Food delivery services

You can also run a food business without having to go through the trouble of starting a restaurant.

The basic idea is to offer to deliver food to people's premises. Today, advances in technology have made it convenient to order in, so much so that many people prefer to have food brought to their doorsteps instead of going to their favorite restaurant, which makes the opportunity to employ yourself by being a food deliverer enormous.

It's worth noting that when it comes to this, there isn't much startup work needed because existing systems make it possible to set up and run this type of business with ease.

Prime examples here include businesses like Uber Eats, SkipTheDishes, Doordash, and others. These companies have already laid out the setup for you: the restaurants, the client-base, and so on. All you have to do is sign-up to the app, meet the requirements, and get ready to receive orders and make deliveries. The more deliveries you make, the more money you make.

Transportation services

Companies like Uber and Lyft have made it relatively easy for anyone with a car and driving skills to run a business providing transport services to the public, thereby earning a decent living doing so.

With this business model, you enjoy the freedom of being the boss, meaning you're the only person responsible for dictating how you use your time. Countless people have found success by being Uber and Lyft drivers. Consider the case of Pierre Hana, a former electronics and communications engineer.

After losing his job to unforeseeable developments in his industry, he started freelancing with Uber. In the beginning, he worked two jobs to supplement his income. Later, the revenue coming from providing Uber services made much more sense to him, and he quit his second job to pursue being a full-time, ride-sharing driver.

If you don't have a job, but you have a car that's just sitting in the driveway, start moonlighting as a freelance driver as you figure things out.

Babysitting

If you not in any current employment, are staying at home with nothing much to do, but you happen to love children, babysitting can prove itself a stellar income opportunity for you.

Picture a mom who has a kid she birthed a few months but has to go to work. Is she in need of someone to take care of her kid? You bet she does, and so do countless other mums in a similar position.

These parents will be willing to trust you with their kids since babysitting is usually cheaper than daycare, which is a selling point in today's economic space where people are trying to stretch a dollar as much as possible.

Babysitting is a very straightforward business to start: all you need to do is start marketing your services immediately. Just talk to people in the neighborhood about your new venture; you might get some leads.

You can also set up a profile at a website like Nextdoor.com and start pitching gigs; you'll find work in no time. Even advertising your services on a website like Craigslist can bear fruits.

The fundamental thing to remember is that, like any client-based business, you want long-term relationships, not one-off gigs. A few well-paying clients are all you need to earn and sustain a good living.

Dog walking

If you like pets, specifically dogs, more than you like kids, you can become a freelance dog walker. As a dog walker, you will offer to keep the dog company, take it out, and inspire new habits.

Dog walking can be a lucrative way to earn money if you don't have any particular aptitudes or academic qualifications: all you need is a passion for dogs.

For the best chance of success, seek clients in upper-middle-class and affluent communities. Such people love their pets; they also have the means to pay someone to take care of their pets.

The story of Jen Tserng, a New York resident and freelance dog walker who CNBC profiled in 2018, might inspire you. At the time, she was earning as much as $60,000 to $80,000 a year from the business. In one particular year, she managed to earn $100,000. What is most inspiring is that she manages to save as much as $40,000 a year. How amazing is that? Who thought a dog walker could manage that?

As this chapter has illustrated, if you are willing to seek unconventional opportunities, there're plenty of ways to create an income stream; you just have to grapple with the bias of occupational status.

You see, too many mainstream professional routes have tough competition detours that will make it harder for you to make a decent living, let alone get a job.

Remember that in the end, a professional status won't pay your bills or help you save for retirement. It's, therefore, better to overcome the crowd mentality and look for means you can use to line your pockets.

Now that you have a healthy list of income-generating ideas that can start you off, in the next section, we shall discuss how you can get started in the world of self-employment:

6

YOUR ULTIMATE GETTING STARTED GUIDE

"An idea not coupled with action will never get any bigger than the brain cell it occupied."

— ARNOLD GLASOW

You've mastered the wealth-building basics, learned how to see things differently, and discovered 45 different possible income sources you could tap into and be well on your way to financial freedom.

All that sounds overwhelming, which can make getting started challenging, which is not what I want because if you don't figure out a way to start putting what you've learned into action, you will get nowhere. All you'll have done is an excellent job of reading this book and acquiring good ideas, but those ideas won't be worth anything to you.

To help ensure you derive the most value from this book, in this section, I'll detail a step-by-step plan that will help you get started:

Step 1: Identify who you are and where you fit in the entrepreneurial world

The world of business is diverse and rich, which, on the one hand, is a good thing because you get to become whoever you want, but which isn't so great on the other hand because if you pursue a path that doesn't fit your personality, the chances of failure are high.

Far too often, people rush into the world of business without considering what suits them, mostly because the prospect of making money causes them to jump into opportunities that are at odds with who they are. Not surprisingly, such people eventually wash out and start a new venture, and guess what, the cycle repeats itself all over again.

Here's the thing you need to know:

In business, no matter what you try to do or who you are, there's nothing like easy money; challenges are numerous and recurring. If you don't love what you do, it won't be long before you give up.

The key to success, therefore, lies in choosing a path that you're likely to keep pursuing during the tough times—and they'll be many—, a path that fills you with passion, not just the greed of money.

That said, here are a few categories of entrepreneurs based on what Robert G. Allen covered in his best-selling book, "Multiple streams of income." Determine where you belong so that you can make wise choices:

Intrapreneur

If you can influence people, persuade them to do something, or lead them down a certain path, you can consider yourself an intrapreneur.

To determine if you're an intrapreneur, ask yourself the questions below. The more "yeses" you have, the likelier your chances of succeeding as an intrapreneur.

- Have you had success influencing other people's decisions?
- Do people seem to take you seriously and pay close attention to what you say?
- Are you outspoken by nature? Have you been able to move a crowd in the past?
- Are you naturally good at selling? Can you tap into people's most pressing desires and sell them an idea or product?

Your ability to convince people to take action makes you great at marketing products and services. Thus, your most promising potential lies in the distribution system that involves making sure products and services reach their intended consumer.

Intrapreneurs make up a disproportionate share of affiliate marketers, network marketers, and digital marketers. They excel at the job because they're good at what they do.

Extrapreneur

You are an extrapreneur if you are the creative type. You are also an extrapreneur if you possess the innate ability to entertain people.

Ask yourself the following:

- Do you (or other people) consider you an artist of sorts?
- Can you engage a crowd?
- Have you ever come up with something useful out of what many would consider nothing or useless junk?

If the above resonates with your personality, you're likely an extrapreneur. What does this realization mean? Well:

Extrapreneurs make for good content creators. They also make good entertainers, designers, inventors, or producers of original art. What is the commonality between all these pursuits? They all require creative talent.

It takes creativity to create a video that will entertain and resonate with people on YouTube. It takes creativity to look at a problem and come up with a tech solution for it. It also takes creativity to come up with a design concept or even some work of art.

Therefore, the three money systems suited to extrapreneurs are content streams, technology streams, as well as aptitude streams. Figure out which one fits your taste and go with it.

Infopreneur

Disseminating valuable information is an infopreneur's strongest suit, and he or she makes money from selling information. To belong to this category, you need to possess unique characteristics.

You need to be a person who loves organizing and simplifying content, as well as deeply passionate about teaching.

Here's your litmus test:

- Do you enjoy teaching other people what you

know? Do you frequently visualize yourself explaining something new to someone?
- Can you break down a complicated topic into its constituent components, thereby making the subject easier to understand?
- Does the idea of contributing to other people's lives excite you?
- Are you good at communicating (both orally and in writing)?
- Do you spend most of your time reading and writing?

If you can answer yes to most of the above questions, you fit the personality profile of an infopreneur.

This category is where I belong—for the most part—because the highlight of my entrepreneurial journey has been creating and selling informational products that help other people—the book you're reading now is as apt an example as any.

I am an introvert by nature and a quiet, cerebral person who is always thinking up ideas and concepts, which means being an infopreneur fits my personality. I have also found that many other successful people in this field have personalities that fit mine to a T.

It takes someone who can read, research, meditate, perceive, and outline, among other things, to create content that can have a lasting effect on peoples' lives.

If you self-designate as an infopreneur, you are better off finding your place in content systems; that's where your potential lies.

Autopreneur

A large number of investors fall under this category or people we can only classify as "analytical types." Analytical types love looking into numbers and can use them to identify opportunities others can't see.

To determine if you have autopreneur tendencies, ask yourself the following questions:

- Are you a frugal person who loves saving money?
- Does the idea of making money while you sleep strike a chord?
- Are you good at finding great bargains and deals?
- Would you like to create automatic income streams that involve little or no hassle?

As you look at these questions, who comes into mind?

Unless you've never heard of him, you no doubt thought of Warren Buffet. The press has widely documented his profile, and he seems to fit the character of an autopreneur.

If you aspire to emulate him, and you are sure that you possess a personality similar to his, look into passive income streams.

I hope these classifications have helped you locate your ideal place in the business world. However, before I move on to the next step, I need to point something out:

Irrespective of where you fit in these categories, technology, as well as freelancing systems, can apply to you —they apply to everyone. Keep that in mind as you decided which income source to pursue.

Step 2: Gather enough information on your area of interest

After discovering where you belong, you need to acquire knowledge on how to operate effectively in your area of expertise. For instance,

If you've discovered that you're well-suited to being a web designer, you need to embark on learning everything you can learn about that niche. Learn the latest design frameworks, current web design trends, project workflows, new design languages, graphic design principles, and so on.

You also need to know how to run your practice, look for clients, qualify clients, the prices to charge, how to negotiate rates, build great client relationships that guarantee repeat assignments, get referrals, which auxiliary services to offer, and so on.

Because change eventually impacts every industry, you also need to stay aware and sharp. You need to anticipate how various developments will impact your bottom-line.

Without enough information, you are likely to struggle to succeed, which makes self-education critical.

When it comes to where to find up to date information, it's tempting to think that college is the answer, but I promise you it isn't. It's too expensive and won't provide you with what you need.

Over the years, I have found that it's easy to find valuable information at a free or low cost. Here are four sources I have found useful:

Google

Your first option is Google, currently the most popular search engine on the planet. With such an enviable reputation, it is the most important source of organic traffic for websites.

The people at Google have made it their business to provide people with accurate and high-quality information from authoritative sources on the internet. That means when you type a query such as "How to start a blog," Google will serve you the most relevant results from experts in the field.

You see:

People around the globe are working hard day and night to write the best and most accurate content so that they can attract organic traffic from Google. That's an advantage because it means that you can find high-quality information on just about every topic you can imagine.

The very act of asking Google a question will most likely lead to a satisfactory answer.

YouTube

Owned by Google, the same company that believes internet users deserve the best content possible, YouTube is an excellent self-learning resource where you can find information on any topic you can imagine, especially if you want tutorials.

If you want resources that take you by the hand and show you every step of the process of doing something, there is no better place to go than YouTube—for free content.

Let's say you want to start a blog with WordPress, you don't have any website design experience, and this is your first time using WordPress. You can learn everything you need to learn from YouTube tutorials.

YouTube has mini-courses on subjects such as cooking, web design, graphic design, programming, Artificial Intelligence, hair styling, tech repairs, social media marketing, and so on.

Just hop over there and make the most of what you find there; how far this one resource takes you will be a surprise.

Podcasts

Because of the hectic nature of the modern world, we have limited reading time. One of the fastest ways to consume valuable content is through audio formats, and these days, podcasts are one of the best places to seek business information and use your idle time productively.

You can listen to a podcast while shopping at the grocery store, navigating through traffic, cooking, doing chores at home, walking outside, and so on.

iTunes features one of the largest collections of podcasts on the web. The great thing about it is that the platform categorizes available podcasts, which makes it easier to find what you need.

Books

Lastly, we have books. If you love reading, books can be good self-learning resources. I especially recommend books because they are comprehensive and detailed.

For Instance, I learned more about content marketing from Joe Pulizzi's Content Inc than from any other source I have ever come across. Likewise, you'll find that if you embrace reading books, you will learn more from them than any other resource. Amazon's kindle store is an awesome reservoir for great books, you can also visit your local library for free resources on any subject.

Step 3: Create instant cash flow by exploring freelance systems

To get started on making money immediately, go the freelancing route because it can help you get the money you need in as little time as possible. The earlier you can start making money, the easier it will be to appreciate what you can accomplish, and the more motivated you shall be to strive for better.

Take the example of a tech guru. You may be good at web development and dream of becoming the CEO of a web development company, providing a premium web-based service. Given this, should you just jump right in with both feet? Of course not.

The odds of short-term success in business are long. It often takes a lot of time before a business can start raking in the "big bucks." While your idea might have merit, you may have to give up midway because of a lack of financial resources with which to support yourself.

The solution is simple: exploit your talents by becoming a freelance web developer, which, as mentioned earlier, is an in-demand skill that pays well. Monetizing this skill will help you pay bills and take care of your short-term needs as you work on your business idea part-time.

Signing up to freelance marketplaces such as Freelancer.com, Upwork.com, Fiverr.com, Peopleperhour.com, and so on, is an effective way to bag quick freelance clients.

Yes, these marketplaces might not be great long-term options because many of them operate on a bidding model, which can disadvantage you as a freelancer, but overall, they're a great way to start earning money fast.

Let me give you an example.

On one of these sites, usually, a client posts a project and an initial starting fee. Then, you and other equally talented experts bid on the price of the project. Most of the time, this results in the price going down. Thus, it's common to find a project that started with an initial fee of $1000 going down to $800 at the moment the client awards it to his or her freelancer of choice.

This fact is one of the reasons why these marketplaces are not attractive to top-quality freelancers. As a freelancer who wants to get paid well, you will want to market yourself to high-paying clients that you find outside such marketplaces.

Additionally, these marketplaces are fiercely competitive, and it's common to find over 100 people bidding on the same project. What are the odds of bagging such a project, especially as a beginner? You know the answer: It's like showing up to an interview that has over 100 possible candidates, many of which have qualifications that overshadow yours. Your chances of making an impression and winning a project are low, if not near zero.

Given their bad reputation, of what value are these sites to you?

Honestly, these sites can help you get started and acquire the experience you need. You will win some low-paying assignments, yes, but ultimately, their importance is beefing up your portfolio and resume. With that, you can feel confident chasing high-paying clients.

Also, these sites help you build some meaningful relationships, which is vital because clients prefer working with the same expert so that they can avoid the hassle of finding someone else.

Thus, by winning a few projects on such platforms, you enhance your chances of getting future assignments. Often, on those other assignments, you can negotiate better rates without involving the platform itself.

Step 4: Identify a challenge you can solve and create a solution

Creating monetizable solutions should be your ultimate goal. Let me explain:

Since I know a lot of people who earn high six figures doing it, I can candidly say that freelancing is a good source of income. However, to gain the financial freedom you want and make the "big bucks," you should find a way to sell a product, provide some kind of automated service, or start an operation that earns money without your active involvement.

Let me use the example of a web developer to illustrate how a service business might work:

Let's say you are a talented web developer who has worked with countless clients and organizations over the years and has spotted a unique market opportunity.

Perhaps you have discovered that your clients are increasingly demanding blockchain technology solutions that fulfill the accounting needs of major players in the financial sector. However, the overhead costs of implementing such changes at an individual business level are prohibitively expensive because of the infrastructure involved.

You've estimated that this technology could also help small and medium scale businesses, and eureka! You have a lightbulb idea. You decide to build a cloud-based accounting platform that utilizes the blockchain technology. Your clients will simply outsource the service to you for a monthly cost of $1000. You estimate that nearly 500 clients will sign up to get the service within the first year. Now your projected revenue is $500,000 each month. Not bad.

Over the next year, you look at how to expand by developing pocket-friendly packages for smaller clients. Once you do that, in a few short years, your revenue will almost double to well over $1,000,000 each month. Now things are getting more interesting since you are looking at a growth market.

You anticipate that pretty soon, you will be netting well close to $50,000,000 each year, and you've only just started. It won't be long before you begin grossing $100,000,000 each year. Then maybe you might decide to issue an IPO so that you tap into a global market or even secure a lucrative exit.

While this idea is hypothetical—and no, you should not assume that you'll achieve success if you start a cloud solutions company—it gives you a fair idea of what's possible. You might come up with a product idea that generates good money, even though it might not run into the hundreds of millions of dollars.

I know of people who have grossed tens of millions of dollars just from selling a single course on Udemy. Some have even gone as far as launching other multiple courses bringing in millions. That could be you one day: all you have to do is embrace the abundance mindset.

Yes, it will take time, and such ideas rarely come to novices, but if you commit to becoming an expert in your chosen field, there's no reason why you can't create a solution that makes you a millionaire.

In the next section, we shall explore how technology can help you build and scale your business:

THE BIGGEST BUSINESS TOOLBOX IN THE WORLD

"As technology advances in complexity and scope, fear becomes more primitive"

— DON DELILLO

Let's talk about technology and the internet. Together they make up the most extensive business toolbox in the entire world. As a smart person, you cannot overlook this toolbox; you must use it to gain every business advantage you can get.

Capitalizing on the internet sounds like a good idea, but doing so can be daunting, and you may not know how to get started, especially if you are not conversant with modern technologies and their uses.

This chapter aims to help you overcome that by giving you ideas detailing how you can implement technology in your business.

Ready? Let's begin.

Enhancing your productivity

Technology can help boost your level of productivity in the following ways:

- **You can rely on time-tracking software to allocate time to various work-related projects.** The most robust software on the market can track the time allocated to your projects and those of your entire staff, meaning you can generate productivity reports for each employee. The benefit of this is that it increases productivity by reducing time wastage. I recommend Clockify and TimeLive.
- **Project management software can help you organize all tasks relating to various business projects.** Dealing with multiple business projects can be a headache, especially if you have to supervise all of them personally. Different Software solutions can help you manage projects and tasks assigned to various

team members, which would help you set business goals and ensure you achieve your business milestones on time. Here, Ayoa and Openproject are ideal solutions.
- **A digital filing system** will help you convert your conventional filing system, such as a cabinet, into a digital one, which will make searching for, editing, sharing, deleting, sorting, and adding new files a breeze. I recommend Laserfiche for this purpose.

Managing finances

You can manage the financial side of your business using the following options:

- **You can use budget-tracking software** to stay on top of your business expenses, which will help you avoid the banality of tracking every expense in your books manually and having to do all that ugly math. You Need A Budget and Mint are by far the best available options for this.
- **You can use professional accounting software** to stay on top of cash flow and your business's financial position. Some software options will allow you to handle and prepare financial statements personally, thereby removing the need for a business accountant. QuickBooks,

Sage, and Banana are some of the best programs for this purpose.
- **For professional financial reporting of**, you can share the raw files generated by accounting programs as well as budgeting software through digital file-sharing platforms such as Google Drive, Microsoft OneDrive, OneHub, eFileCabinet, DropBox, and the like.

Marketing

Marketing is the engine that supports any business. Thankfully, technology— and the internet—offer countless options here too:

- **You can establish an online presence** by setting up a website, which puts your business profile out there for other people to browse and find out about your products and services.
- **You can use Business Planning Software** such as LivePlan to nail down a well-thought-out marketing plan that guides and centralizes your business's marketing efforts in your business. You can then share this plan with concerned parties within your business.
- **You can also leverage the power of digital marketing** through social media platforms like Facebook, Twitter, LinkedIn, Instagram, Snapchat, Pinterest, etc. These platforms make

it possible to advertise your products and services to millions, even billions of people around the world. It is important to point out that each of these platforms has unique marketing best practices. You will need to search for training programs that will help you master marketing and advertising on your platform of choice. Adespresso.com is a nice place to start because it offers marketing guides for Facebook, Instagram, Twitter, and Google Ads.

- **You can also start a content resource for your ideal audience;** you can monetize this resource later. As mentioned earlier in this book, a blog on your website can be an excellent way to accomplish this.
- **You can also leverage the power of email marketing.** In the past, direct mail was one of the most effective ways to market to well-defined audiences. Today, email has taken the place of that medium. You probably receive mail from businesses earmarked as Promotions, Updates, and so on. That form of marketing is very effective and cost-friendly. You can build an email list of prospects list by integrating lead magnets and opt-in forms on your blog or landing page. One of the best strategies is to offer something valuable—lead

magnet—in exchange for a name and email address.

- **Video marketing is also an attractive option.** The demand for video content, especially on the internet, is impressive. Video content also gets more shares, has higher conversion rates than most other types of content, and is one of the most effective marketing strategies on any platform. You can use your smartphone camera to film videos, create presentations using software such as PowerPoint, or create animation videos—you can hire someone on Fiverr.com for this.

Make learning and sharing ideas easier

Learning and sharing ideas within the business is crucial for long-term survival and success. Here are some ways technology can help with that:

- You can use video or web conferencing software to hold virtual meetings. Today, conferencing software supports features such as real-time video and audio, instant messaging features, file-sharing features, as well as screen sharing. In other words, face-to-face contact whenever you need to hold meetings or convey messages to a group of people is no longer necessary, which is especially important now

that we are all practicing social distancing. Examples of video conferencing software options that can broadcast real-time content via the web include Skype, Zoom, Cisco Webex, Agora.io, Microsoft teams, Adobe Connect, and Google Hangouts.
- As for training, you can acquire credentials and licenses that give your employees access to online education platforms such as Udemy, Coursera, Edx.org, Skillshare, MIT OpenCourseWare, etc. One these platforms, you will get access to updated course material on various areas of interest that can help your business. If team members want to share and compare notes, you can use file-sharing platforms like Google Drive, Dropbox, OneDrive, and so on.

Improve Customer Service

Technology can also improve how you interact with your customers. For instance, you can do the following:

- You can rely on social media to gather intelligence on your customers so that you can serve them better. With Facebook, for example, you can create a group where customers raise and discuss various issues regarding your product or service. You can rely on the

discussions to determine where you could improve as a business or come up with new product ideas.
- Another excellent approach is to set up an online help desk. One of the most successful examples of this is an online chat widget placed on the main website. In more sophisticated business operations where customers can raise multiple issues, a ticketing system can help track customer inquiries and ensure satisfactory resolution of their issues.
- If you run a service-based business, such as a doctor, lawyer, massage parlor, consultancy, therapy, and so on, you typically employ an appointment-based model. Instead of going at it the old-fashioned way, you can implement a digital appointment-scheduling system that lets your customers do the job themselves. Calendly is a software that helps your clients to book appointments with you seamlessly.
- What if you want feedback from your customers or would-be customers for that matter? In that case, you can run a survey or questionnaire. Google Forms, TypeForm, and SurveyMonkey all allow you to create forms designed to collect user input in classical survey fashion.

Remote Administration

Last but not least, you can use technology to support remote work. If so, here are a few ways you can accomplish that:

- You can acquire a remote desktop application that lets you log in to your workstation from a remote location, thus making it possible to complete work as if you're sitting at your work desk, even though you may be far, far away. TeamViewer has such capabilities. Other such tools include LogMeIn Pro, VNC Connect, Zoho Assist, AnyDesk, and ConnectWise Control. You will have to find one that suits your particular taste and needs.
- You can use your smartphone to receive and make phone calls, yes, but also to connect to the cloud so that you can view and make changes to documents and other file types—apps like Google Drive, OneDrive, and Dropbox.

You can adopt at least a handful of these technologies and apply them to your business. When you do that, you will have an easier time running your business.

In the next chapter, we shall talk about ways and means to handle the money your business generates.

8

WEALTH ACCUMULATION, WEALTH PRESERVATION, & WEALTH TRANSFER

"If we command our wealth, we shall be rich and free. If our wealth commands us, we are poor indeed."

— EDMUND BURKE

With money, the most important thing is what you do with it once you have it. Any fool can make money; it takes a wise man to keep and grow it.

The ideas we have discussed so far are excellent generators of money and wealth. If you implement at least one path to the latter, you will make money, with the amount depending on your effort.

Once you have the money in your hands, what do you do with it? This question is one you need to answer long before you make money: you need to have a "money plan" in place before the money starts rolling in.

Making a plan once the money is in your hands is a bad idea because the presence of money makes you euphoric, too "high" to make objective money choices. A lack of objectivity leads you to financial decisions that will hurt you in the long run.

Think about it:

People make—money sometimes a lot of money—all the time. Yet, why are so few people genuinely wealthy? The simple answer is that people usually give in to the temptation to use their money on the wrong things.

Once money comes into your hands, you tend to feel a rush that compels you to go out and spend it on something, to spoil yourself a little, or invest in risky investment vehicles that promise quick returns. All sorts of bad things happen when you have unplanned-for money in your hands. The best way to hedge against that is to create a sensible plan.

Here are a few key things you can do to put your money to good use once it starts coming in:

Reinvesting in your business

We've heard many times before that wealth comes from investing. By many assessments, this assumption is very right.

However, this assumption also begs the question:

> Where exactly should you invest a large portion of your money? Is it stocks, bonds, real estate, or certificates of deposit?

If you guessed any of the above, you would be wrong. The safest place to pack the biggest portion of your money is in your area of expertise. If your business is generating a good sum of money consistently, then you're an expert at running it. Otherwise, you wouldn't be generating consistent revenue from it.

Don't get me wrong. Plenty of wealthy people invest in stocks, bonds, currencies, commodities, and various other popular investment vehicles. There is nothing special about these people.

The reason they've become wealthy through such means is that they are experts at what they do. They've studied; and continue to master their game year after year. That's why they make the kind of money that they do.

The average person could never expect to generate the returns they get from what they do. The average person, with limited knowledge about speculative investments, can only hope for returns of about 10% in any given year.

The truth is that the average person has no business speculating. Instead, such a person should consult a fnancial advisor, portfolio manager, CPA, or another related professional.

If you buy some stock expectation that its value will triple in the next few years but end up losing all your money, the only person you have to blame is yourself. That is what happens to people who try to get into a risky venture they have no business getting into because of a lack of expertise.

The wise thing to do is to reinvest the profits you earn into your business. If you are a freelancer, invest in marketing yourself and upgrading your knowledge so that you can get more and better clients and charge higher rates. If you run an online store, invest in digital marketing, and acquiring additional stock.

Invest in the area you know well. That is the best and safest investment decision you could ever make.

Savings and investments

What should you do when you have an excess amount of cash? For instance, what if you are one of the highest-earning doctors in the world, you're earning an income other doctors envy, and don't wish to start a private practice?

What if you've reasonably invested the most you can in your business, and injecting additional capital into your business would be nothing short of wasteful? What should you do then?

If you ever face such a scenario, then saving and investing in speculative vehicles, or other common and more conservative ones like real estate will be the most logical thing to do.

You may choose to purchase a mutual fund, an index fund, an ETF, or even a piece of commercial real estate. At this point, you have every reason to do so; otherwise, your money would simply go to waste.

Before you do this, however, seek the counsel of an expert, or perform your due diligence first. There are more bad investment opportunities than there are good ones, and it only takes a single decision born out of impatience or ignorance to reverse any financial gains you may have made.

Always remember this: the very fact that you've invested in a specific vehicle doesn't mean your investment is safe or that returns are a guarantee.

Wealth preservation

What if your goal is to preserve the wealth you've attained?

What if you've achieved your ultimate financial and wealth goals, and you no longer wish to take significant risks in search of greater investment returns?

What if you've just received a sudden windfall that puts more money in your laps than you know what to do with it?

What if you want the money you've made to outlast you by more than one generation? What if you're a retiree who doesn't want to subject his/her money to significant ups and downs in the financial markets?

If you have any of these goals, you will want to employ a different financial strategy, one that focuses on capital preservation. You will probably only want to earn a small return that will help you minimize the effects of:

- Taxes
- Inflation
- Capital market fluctuations

Given these objectives, what vehicles are best? I have two in mind:

Annuities

An annuity is a contract drawn between you and an insurance company. The contract usually obligates the insurance company to pay you an agreed sum at regular intervals either immediately or at some specified point in the future. You can schedule the periodic payments to be made monthly, quarterly, semi-annually or annually. It can be for a specific period, such as 30 years, or for the rest of your life.

The contract also obligates you to make deposits to the insurance company upfront, either as a lump sum or as a series of payments.

The good thing about an annuity is that it ties up your money, allowing you to spend it responsibly without squandering it or getting tempted to make some risky financial choices.

Guaranteed Investment Funds

A Guaranteed Investment Fund (GIF) also known as segregated fund is another product offered by Insurance companies.

This product allows you to invest in financial markets such as stocks, bonds, index funds, and so on, but with minimal risk. It also guarantees you a specific sum when the fund matures or when you die.

Some GIFs also offer the option to reset the guaranteed amount to a higher value should your portfolio experience a significant upswing.

The feature that makes GIFs attractive as a great wealth preservation tool is the guaranteed amount, which guarantees that your wealth will not disappear because of some giant mistake or unforeseen event.

Life insurance and wealth transfer

Eventually when life ends, you may wish to transfer your wealth to family, close relatives, or some other beneficiary such as your favorite charity. Many strategies can work for that purpose, but one of the easiest ones is to take out a life insurance policy.

A life insurance policy is a contract drawn between you and an insurance company, obligating the insurance company to pay a death benefit to a beneficiary in the event of your death. Your obligation, on the other hand, is to pay a premium over a certain period. A death benefit is the amount of money the insurance company promises in the contract to disburse to the beneficiary tax free.

A life insurance policy can also be a unique wealth accumulation tool as some policies are designed with some investment components. Permanent life insurance plans such as Whole life and universal life plans are an hybrid of insurance and investments, thus useful as a family wealth protection tool as well as a wealth accumulation tool if taken early in life.

Worth noting is that before you take the policy, the insurance company will investigate your health to determine if you are a risk worthy candidate. Additionally, the insurance company will investigate the circumstances of your death. For instance, life insurance does not cover death by suicide if this happens within the first few years of the contract.

Estate Planning

While wealth transfer options like life insurance sound simple enough, it has some limitations, It pays a lumpsum to your beneficiaries upon death but it doesn't necessarily coordinate your affairs after your demise.

You need to put your house in order by creating a Will and/or a Power of Attorney

 A Will is a legal document determining the distribution of property and belongings after a person's death.

What if you suddenly fall ill and can't look after your affairs? This is when a Power of Attorney comes to life.

A power of attorney (POA) is a legal document giving a person chosen by you the power to act on your behalf. This person may have broad legal authority or limited authority to make legal decisions about your property, finances or medical care. The power of attorney would be used if you become indisposed due to an illness or disability, or in case you can't be present to sign necessary legal documents for financial transactions.

The Onus lies on you to ensure a seamless process of wealth transfer, you should seek estate planning services from a professional such as an estate attorney.

Estate planning will assure you of the following:

- Asset dispersion among beneficiaries as per your wishes
- Speedy execution of your estate
- You create a plan detailing who will manage what should you fall severely ill
- Reduced the tax burden levied on your estate upon your death
- Reduced death associated costs
- You can choose an estate executor

Since you don't want to forgo these benefits, my final recommendation is to seek the services of a professional estate planner.

CONCLUSION

Thanks for staying with me throughout this book.

We've covered plenty so far. We've talked about the need for a change in mentality, about embracing change gracefully, money fundamentals, basic money systems, and looked at different money streams you can pursue.

We've also addressed the issue of falling into the trap of consumerism and the wealthy-building impediments it presents.

We've talked about technology and the various ways you can use it to improve your business. We've also discussed steps you can take to make sure the money you generate from all your efforts doesn't just disappear into thin air—or uninformed investment choices.

I admit it's a lot to take in, yes, but the beauty is that this material is life-changing. Perhaps, after reading this book, your life will never be the same; it may change for the better, if you commit to taking action.

You now have all the tools you need to have to take control of your financial destiny. Nothing or no one is stopping you, just yourself.

You cannot read a book about losing weight and then leave the exercises to someone else. Practice what you've learned, for knowledge without application is totally useless.

I hope you've received great value from reading this book. If that's the case, imparting this knowledge was an honor and every effort that went into creating this book was worth it.

If you enjoyed this book, I would appreciate an honest Amazon review. If you would like me to write a book specifically on a particular money system or on any other topic, I would be glad to read suggestions from you. My contact email address is moa@thejoblessmillionaire.com.

Let me also wish you all best as you embark on your journey to financial independence and ultimately financial freedom.

DISCUSSION SECTION

Here are a few things worth mentioning:

- Building wealth is not a matter of how much you make per se. It has more to do with how much you keep and how well you invest whatever you keep.
- If you make a lot of money but spend all of it, then you will never accumulate wealth or achieve financial freedom.
- Between now and the moment you die, life will undergo all sorts of changes. Do not fear the change. Just be willing to learn and accept whatever is going on around you. If you lean into change, you'll be fine.
- If you want a secure financial future, don't be comfortable with surrendering control of your

career and dignity to someone else. You must be the captain of your ship, and boldly set a course you want to follow.
- Success in business is about discovering an opportunity, testing it to verify your conclusions, and then going all in.
- If you want success at selling, start by creating content that attracts and engages an audience.
- The best place to invest your money is where you have the most knowledge and expertise. Often, that place is your business or professional practice.

www.ingramcontent.com/pod-product-compliance
Lightning Source LLC
Chambersburg PA
CBHW020648220526
45464CB00001B/337